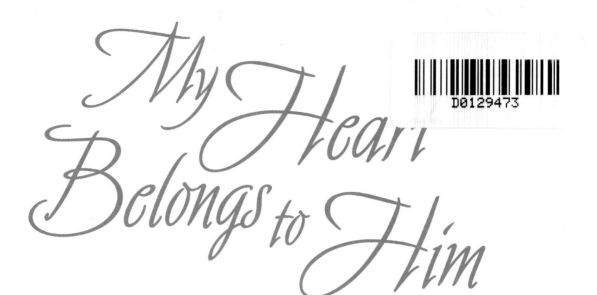

My Heart Belongs to Him —My Identity

An Interactive Study
to Prepare for
Courageous
Womanhood

Mother's Guide

Nancy Butkowski and Leslie J. Barner

FAMILYLIFE™
Bringing Timeless Principles Home

Little Rock, Arkansas

My Heart Belongs to Him—My Identity, Mother's Guide

Published by FamilyLife, a division of Campus Crusade for Christ.

Authors: Nancy Butkowski and Leslie J. Barner
Senior Editor: David Boehi
Editorial Team: Robert Anderson, Ben Colter, Mary Larmoyeux, and Susan Matthews
Cover Design: Chuck Bostwick
Photography: Willie Allen
Interior Layout: Claes Jonasson
Illustrations: Steve Björkman

ISBN 1-57229-264-4

Printed in the United States of America.

Most of the content of Knowing God Personally in the appendix is excerpted from *Would You Like to Know God Personally?* a version of *Have You Heard of the Four Spiritual Laws?* (written by Bill Bright). Copyright © 1965, 1968 by Campus Crusade for Christ, Inc. All rights reserved.

Unless otherwise noted, Scripture references are taken from the *New American Standard Bible®*. Copyright © 1960, 1962, 1963, 1971, 1972, 1973, 1975, 1977 by the The Lockman Foundation. Used by permission.

Other Scripture quotations are from:
The Holy Bible, New International Version®. NIV®. Copyright © 1973, 1978, 1984 by International Bible Society. Used by permission of Zondervan Publishing House. All rights reserved.

The Living Bible (TLB) © 1971. Used by permission of Tyndale House Publishers, Inc., Wheaton, IL. All rights reserved.

J.B. Phillips' *The New Testament in Modern English* © 1958, 1960, 1972. All rights reserved.

FAMILYLIFE™
Bringing Timeless Principles Home

Dennis Rainey, Executive Director
3900 North Rodney Parham Road
Little Rock, AR 72212-2441
(501) 223-8663
1-800-FL-TODAY
www.familylife.com

A division of Campus Crusade for Christ

Dedication

For my mom, Mildred Johnson, who directed my heart
toward Christ and encouraged me to live my life in a way
that would bring honor and glory to God.

NB

For my mom, Geraldine Noble, who encouraged me to
put Christ first in all things through her faithful prayers,
godly example, and wise advice over the years.

LJB

Table of Contents

Daughter's Guide

Foreword

Congratulations! Moms and daughters, you are about to embark on an exciting journey as you travel through the pages of *My Heart Belongs to Him—My Identity*. This practical study will knit your hearts together as you consider biblical principles that build godly character.

It wasn't too long ago when my daughters and I sat where you are sitting—sharing heart to heart—passing values from one generation to the next. I am now finishing the miles of my full-time mothering years as our daughter Ashley begins her journey as a mother. I cherish the one-on-one talks that I had with Ashley and the other girls, hoping they would avoid many of the mistakes that I made.

As I shared God's wisdom with each of my daughters, I was reminded of how our Lord wants His truth and practical advice to be passed from one generation to another. Nancy Butkowski and Leslie Barner have crafted a wonderful book that does just that. It opens the doors of communication between mothers and daughters and helps build life-long friendships.

I think you would agree that there is no substitute for a mother's love. And there is no greater joy than for a mother to know that her daughter's heart belongs completely to Jesus Christ ... that together their hearts belong to Him!

Barbara Rainey

Mother and Daughter Testimonials

My Heart Belongs to Him *has been a vehicle that God has used to strengthen my relationship with my daughter. It has provided an avenue to face tough issues and resolve them biblically.*

Ellen Monroe

Through this study it became clear to me that I should have a growing relationship with God before I have any deep relationships with girls or guys. My security must be in God, and not in who I'm with or what I look like.

Kaitlin Monroe

This is the best material I have ever seen anywhere on friendships, relationships, conflict resolution, and purity! If I could choose only one study to do with my daughter—this would be the one! In my opinion, there is nothing else out there with this level of quality, depth, and practicality.

Frances Bradley

This book was eye-opening. It made me think about issues on dating and relationships in ways I have never thought about before.

Beth Bradley

Every mother wants to connect with her teenage daughter in a meaningful way. My Heart Belongs to Him *is an excellent tool to help reach this goal and create a strong bond for the years ahead. Its practical, biblically based perspective on relationships deals soundly with the questions and choices facing teenagers. As my daughter and I used this wonderful study, I was able to see her stresses, as well as become better equipped to provide the support she needs during this time of her life.*

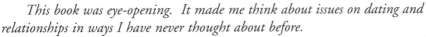

Linda Scholl

I am very grateful that I was able to go through this material when I was in the 6th grade and then again when I was in junior high. It helped me to think not only about issues I'm dealing with now, but also things I may be facing in the future. This study taught me what my goals should be as a Christian girl in areas like friendships, dating, and family. It also helped me to sort out what my dating standards are going to be as I enter high school.

Lindsey Scholl

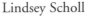

It was enlightening to observe my daughter's responses to the topics presented, and fun to see her formulate her plan of action for situations that might arise in her life. It was a privilege to guide her along the path toward becoming a godly young woman.

Deborah Beuerman

This was an awesome study that every teenage girl should have the opportunity to go through. Now that I have had time to think about what it means to be a godly woman of courage, I am much more prepared to decide what I would do in various situations. In our small group setting, it was helpful to have role-playing and discussion so that I could see other points of view, learn from them, and begin applying changes to my own life.

Molly Beuerman

I enjoyed the study for teenage girls and their mothers held at our church. I was particularly interested in the section that encouraged teens to do things together in groups rather than pairing off and dating. As a mother of a teenager, and a Christian, I also appreciated the foundation of God's Word in this program.

Jan Rogers

My mom and I seemed to bond through this experience and now we know each other better. I never realized what a big deal dating is. I knew it was wrong to have sex before marriage, but I had never known there were verses in the Bible to back this up. The Bible and this study addressed many other issues in my life too. I learned about setting standards and about staying in groups with the guys instead of going out one-on-one. I know so much more about love and dating now that I have been through this course.

Leslie Rogers

This is a great way to talk about things with your daughter. It really helped us look at issues together, communicate better, and grow to know each other more deeply.

Lacey Nielson

I really appreciated the options that this study pointed out to me, many of which I had never considered. Many of the questions really made me stop and think about my attitudes and decisions.

Stephanie Nielson

My Heart Belongs to Him — My Identity

Mother's Guide

GETTING STARTED

Chapter 1

What Is the Purpose of This Study?

Do you remember when you were a teenager—that in-between age, when you felt you were too old to be considered a child, and your parents felt you were too young to be considered an adult? Do you remember wanting to be trusted with independence, yet challenged every day with making right choices against the strong waves of peer pressure? And there were the pressing issues you faced … to drink or not to drink, dating, drugs, sex, friendships, make-up, keeping up with the styles, fitting in, and others.

Adolescence can be a trying time for young women. These are the years when young women experience many life changes physically, emotionally, spiritually, and socially. For many, it's a time when they move from family dependency to peer dependency, looking more to their friends for answers and relying on them as confidants. It's a time when young women may need their parents' love and wise counsel the most.

Without the close guidance of their parents, many young women fall prey to a morally declining culture—a culture that screams, "No limits!" "No rules!" and "Just do it!" As a result, young women of all ages, backgrounds, and ethnicity are struggling with low self-esteem, the consequences of pre-marital sex, broken friendships, broken relationships, hurt, disappointment, depression, eating disorders, and more.

In response to the need for parental involvement and guidance in adolescence, FamilyLife has created a two-book series entitled *My Heart Belongs to Him*. *My Identity* is the subtitle and focus for this book, and *Relating With Others* is the subtitle and focus for the other book. The series is designed to help mothers build solid relationships with their daughters (ages 11-16), while teaching them biblical values that will build character and prepare them for courageous womanhood. Courageous womanhood is having the courage to become the women God created them to be— physically, mentally, emotionally, socially, and especially spiritually.

My Heart Belongs to Him provides a creative way to open the lines of communication between mothers and daughters through an atmosphere of trust. It can also be easily adapted to small groups (such as home Bible study groups, youth groups, and Sunday school classes) to equip teenage girls to make right choices during the challenging adolescent years.

We hope this study will help strengthen the relationship between you and your daughter, as you guide her in making wise choices and in establishing a growing, intimate relationship with the Lord. May she, and other young women who go through this study, develop godly character and make an impact on their world for Christ.

What Is This Study Intended to Accomplish?

Young women who participate in these sessions will find that the experience:

- Allows them to interact with their mothers on a regular basis and on an intimate level, opening the lines of meaningful communication and building a close relationship and a life-long friendship

- Stimulates them to examine what Scripture says about the various issues teens face

- Helps them to grow and mature as an individual and in their relationships with the Lord

- Equips them to make wise choices for godly living in their everyday lives

- Motivates them to influence others and to make an impact on their world for Christ

Can This Study Be Used in Other Settings Besides Mother/Daughter One-On-One?

Yes! With good leadership skills and a heart to help young women grow in character and wisdom, make right choices, and impact their world for Christ, this study may be used effectively in other settings. For example:

- A **single father** could use it with his daughter. Dad may want to involve a female mentor, such as a relative or family friend, in the process of training his daughter in areas directly related to female issues.

- A woman could use this study to mentor a **small group** of young women and their mothers. It's a great way for mothers to get together and train their daughters alongside their peers. In this setting mothers gain support, encouragement, and practical approaches to various issues from one another.

- A grandmother or other **female relative** could use it to mentor a granddaughter, niece, etc.

- A female **youth leader** or **Sunday school** teacher could adapt it to a larger group setting for girls ages 11-16.

There will be girls who do not have a mother to take them through *My Heart Belongs to Him*. This is a significant ministry opportunity for an aunt, grandmother, or other relative to step in and mentor this young lady. In addition, godly women who are friends of the family could also take the challenge of mentoring a young woman (or a small group of young women). You will need to explain to a girl in this situation that the guides use the words "daughter" and "mother" often, but that you are adapting this material so that you can participate with her and invest in her life.

A special word for adoptive mothers or stepmothers: There are additional relational challenges for you as an adoptive mother or stepmother in using this interactive study with your daughter. Even if you do not refer to each other as mother and daughter, remind your young woman that God has a special plan for your family and has blessed your life and your home with her. Communicate how much you care about her and that you are using this study to help her to be all God intended. God Himself set the model for adoption (or step-parenting). It's one of His greatest gifts (see Galatians 4:5-7).

Does Each Session Follow a Format?

Yes. The following outline gives a quick look at how the sessions are structured:

- **Get Ready**—An introduction to the topic that includes the key Scripture, a fictional story, and related discussion questions

- **Get Real**—An overview of the topic, which gives your daughter "the big picture" as it is in our world today

- **Get Direction** — A Bible discovery section

- **Get Going** — The life application section of each chapter

- **Keep Moving** — Additional projects designed to help your daughter deepen her experience as she works through this study

Two special sections are also included throughout each session:

- **Let's Talk About It** — Built-in discussion times for mother and daughter designed to help open the lines of communication

- **Let's Pray About It** — Built-in prayer times for mother and daughter, designed to draw you closer to God and to each other

What Time Schedule Should We Plan to Follow?

The material is not dated so you can work through the study with your daughter at your own pace and according to your schedule. Each session is designed to be covered in two 60-minute sessions or one 90-minute session. Therefore, if you meet weekly and complete the entire session at each meeting, the study can be completed in 8 weeks (or in 16 weeks if you meet every other week). However if you desire to move at a slower pace, with shorter meeting times, you can complete the first half of a session in one meeting and then complete the second half of that session in your next meeting. With this schedule you can complete the study in 16 weeks meeting weekly or in 32 weeks meeting every other week.

For your convenience, we have added a suggested breaking point (designated by the stop sign) in each session if you would prefer to divide the session into two meetings. Depending on your daughter's needs, you can spend more time on some sessions, spend less on others, and determine where in the session to stop. Your decision should be based upon the significance of the subject matter in each session as it relates to your daughter's life and unique needs.

How Is the Bible Used in This Study?

This study presents the Bible as the final authority on life issues and as The Guidebook for daily living and making right choices. Although written centuries ago, the Bible is the most up-to-date book there is, speaking clearly and powerfully about the conflicts and struggles people face. Relevant for all ages, God's Word contains His instructions for dealing with the day-to-day issues of life.

The main Bible translation used throughout the study is the New American Standard, unless otherwise indicated. You may want to use a "Parallel Bible" (with several versions) to work through some of the Bible studies in the sessions.

What About the *Mother's Guide?*

The *Mother's Guide* is easy-to-use. It contains everything you need to lead your daughter successfully in this study. No preparation is needed, however you may want to review the content of each session before you get together with your daughter. When you meet, begin your time together with prayer. ***Then read through the session paragraph by paragraph taking turns reading aloud, pausing for designated discussion and prayer times.***

The *Mother's Guide* contains the same content as the *Daughter's Guide*, with additional helps and tips for you to use to take your daughter to a deeper level of understanding. You will find that your book and your daughter's book correspond with each other by page number. At the beginning of each session, the focus and the objectives for that session are provided to introduce you to the content, and give you an overview of what your daughter will be learning. Throughout each session, you will discover additional helps or tips to give you insight about the content. Suggested answers to certain discussion questions are also provided to enhance your mother/daughter talks.

Chapter 2   KICKING OFF THE STUDY

Enjoy an Evening of Challenge

Create a special evening of challenge for your daughter as a lead-in to the study! You may want to take her to her favorite restaurant or ice-cream shop and introduce the material to her there. Here are some tips for this important evening.

- Tell your daughter that she has a unique opportunity to talk with you one-on-one about the issues and challenges that she will face in her teenage and young adult years.

- Explain to your daughter the importance of preparing herself for courageous womanhood.

- Explain to your daughter how the study will help her to set godly standards for her life and equip her for making wise choices.

- Share with her how the study will equip her to influence her peers to make wise choices and help her to challenge them to an intimate relationship with Christ and godly living.

- Give her the *Daughter's Guide* and ask her to review it, especially the introduction and the testimonials from other young women her age.

- Point out the contents of the book and the topics that the two of you will explore together. Show her the features of the book, including the fictional short stories and the interactive prayer and discussion times.

- Discuss with her how often you plan to meet, and the length of time it will take to complete your study together.

- Remind her that this will be an adventure that the two of you will enjoy together.

- Make it clear that completing the study will be challenging, but it will be a lot of fun and worth the effort.

- Explain that if she completes the study you will honor her accomplishment with a special celebration and a special gift (recognizing her accomplishment and her becoming a courageous young woman).

Ask your daughter to think and pray about your challenge and give her a firm starting date and time. Make sure that you present the program in such a way that your daughter will be excited and motivated, and will look forward to your meeting together as mother and daughter to work through the material.

Please Read This Before You Get Started!

My Heart Belongs to Him was written for Christian pre-teens and teenagers. Many of the awesome promises quoted from the Bible apply to those who love Jesus and know Him as their personal Savior and Lord. In Jeremiah 29:12-13 God tells us, "Then you will call upon Me and come and pray to Me, and I will listen to you. You will seek Me and find Me when you search for Me with all your heart." This is a God who is interested in having a close personal relationship with us. If your daughter has not yet received Jesus Christ as Savior and Lord of her life, we have provided information in the appendix entitled, "You Can Know God Personally," to help you share the good news of what Jesus has made possible with her before you begin the study. However, do not try to force her to make a decision to accept Christ if she is not ready. Instead, prayerfully take her through the study. The discussion topics will apply to her life, and hearing what God says about these real-life issues may prepare her heart to receive the Lord. As you take this life-changing journey together, remember to pray for your daughter faithfully. Look for opportunities to lovingly share your faith and point her toward the Savior.

Chapter 3 — THE CELEBRATION CEREMONY

Planning a Ceremony for Individuals

Upon completion of this study, we suggest that you host a celebration ceremony in your daughter's honor. A special, formal family dinner at home is one suggested setting. Another option is a dinner hosted or catered in some unique setting. You may want to invite extended family members and friends, or keep it intimate with immediate family only. A suggested format for the ceremony is outlined below. As the highlight of the ceremony, you may want to present your daughter with a Purity Pledge and a special ring, bracelet, necklace, or locket to symbolize her commitment to purity and to give Christ first place in everything (see Colossians 1:18b).

Ceremony Outline:

1. Dinner

2. Introduction (see sample "Opening Words for Mom")

3. Words from daughter on the topic, "What I've Gained from this Study"

4. Presentation of Dad's Letter (see "Guidelines for the Letters ... ")

5. Presentation of Mom's Letter (see "Guidelines for the Letters ... ")

6. Words from siblings (either prepared verbally or in a letter)

7. Presentation of the Purity Pledge (see "Sample Purity Pledge") and signing of the pledge

8. Presentation of the symbolic piece of jewelry (ring, bracelet, necklace, locket, etc.) by Dad and/or Mom

9. Special prayer (by the family for the daughter's protection, wisdom, and direction)

Planning a Ceremony for Groups

Upon completion of this study, we suggest that you host a celebration ceremony to honor the girls. A church or selected banquet hall would be a good setting. You may want to invite extended family members and friends of the group, or keep it intimate with immediate family members only. A suggested format for the ceremony is outlined below. As the highlight of the ceremony, you may want each of the girls' parents to present their daughters with a Purity Pledge and a special ring, bracelet, necklace, or locket to symbolize their commitment to purity and to give Christ first place in everything (see Colossians 1:18b).

Ceremony Outline:

1. Dinner (optional)

2. Introduction to the ceremony: special words from the group leader regarding the group's completion of the study

3. Words from the girls (one or two sentences on the topic "What I've Gained from this Study")

4. Words (letters) from each mom and dad (see "Guidelines for the Letters ...")

5. Presentation of the Purity Pledge said in unison (see "Sample Purity Pledge") and signing of the pledges

6. Presentation of the symbolic piece of jewelry (ring, bracelet, necklace, locket, etc.) by each dad and/or mom

7. Stand in family groups for special prayer. Each family will pray for their daughters' protection, wisdom, and direction. The father of each group (mother, if single) should lead in prayer.

8. Reception to follow (if dinner was not served) with cake, punch, and fellowship

Samples

Opening Words for Mom:

(Feel free to use the following sample or to use your creativity to make your opening words even more personal as you bless and honor your daughter on this special day.)

Thank you for sharing in our celebration to honor (your daughter's name) for the completion of *My Heart Belongs to Him—My Identity.* I remember clearly what it was like to be a teenager—the "in-between age." I remember when I felt too old to be considered a child, and yet I was too young to be considered an adult. I too wanted independence, yet the responsibility connected with that independence seemed overwhelming. I remember facing those tough issues that teenagers face: to drink or not to drink, drugs, sex, friendships, make-up, keeping up with the styles, fitting in, and so on. To say the least, the teen years are extremely challenging. It takes courage grounded in God's truth to make the kind of choices that will not only guard your own heart, but also influence the hearts of others.

As (your daughter's name) and I have addressed many of these issues we have found that our feelings are very similar. We have enjoyed our time together interacting about biblical values that will help to build her character and prepare her for *courageous womanhood.* She has learned that this means having the courage to become the woman that God has created her to be physically, mentally, emotionally, socially, and especially spiritually.

This study has helped us grow closer to each other and to God through our special times of learning, sharing, and discovering together. I have watched (your daughter's name) grow in the Lord and in personal maturity as we prayed together, studied together, discussed the issues, and explored the importance of honoring God in our everyday choices and decisions. I have enjoyed watching (your daughter's name) make a daily effort to put the biblical principles she has learned into practice in her everyday life.

And so, it is with great joy that we set aside today to celebrate (your daughter's name), and the great work that God is doing in her life as a result of her faithfulness and the completion of this study. Thank you for being here. We hope that you enjoy celebrating this special occasion with us.

Guidelines for the Letters From Mom and Dad to Your Daughter [1]

These letters are to be written individually, one from Mom and one from Dad. The purpose of the letters is to provide your daughter with personalized words of appreciation for her accomplishments and growth through this study. You will also offer her words of encouragement and words of wisdom as she begins to live out what she's learned. (If you are a single parent, you might ask a close family member or adult friend to write and present the second letter.) These letters are to be presented to your daughter upon completion of the study, and they can be read aloud at your celebration ceremony. Undoubtedly, your daughter will read these letters time and time again, and she will treasure them always.

Below, you will find some guidelines to help you write the letters. If, for some reason, you feel that you really cannot write the letters, please don't worry. There are no references to these letters in the *Daughter's Guide*. At the ceremony, in place of the letters, you may choose to verbally appreciate and encourage your daughter to acknowledge her accomplishments and growth throughout the study without an accompanying letter.

1. Preparation

- Before you write your letter, spend some time thinking about and praying for your daughter—how God worked in her life throughout the study, how she has grown and matured, what you appreciate about her (include her God-given gifts, talents, and strengths), and why she makes you proud. Also think through and pray about what words of wisdom you want to share with your daughter to challenge her to live out the biblical principles she has learned for making wise choices in her life.

- Take notes and make these the basis for your letter.

- You may find it helpful to discuss your observations with your spouse, a grandparent, or a friend who knows your child well.

2. Writing the Letter

- **Draft:** Using your notes, write out a rough draft of your letter on a separate sheet. Then when you have the letter the way you want it, rewrite it on a special piece of stationery that your daughter can treasure always (if you desire and have the necessary tools or resources, you might prefer to have it typed on a computer in a special font).

- **Personal:** Share your feelings in a natural way. This needs to be your own style of communicating.

- **A Milestone:** Recognize that she is growing up and that completing this study is a big step toward courageous womanhood. Indicate that she is becoming a young woman and that you are excited about her teen years, as well as God's plans for her future.

- **Appreciation:** Share how proud you are of her and let her know how much you appreciate her.

- **Affirmation:** Highlight her God-given uniqueness and some key gifts, talents, and strengths that you see God developing in her life.

- **Mission:** Remind her that God has created her with a unique purpose and mission in life. Explain that her God-given gifts, talents, and strengths (along with her sincere desire to love and serve God and others) are key to fulfilling her mission.

- **Commitment and Love:** Indicate that, with the power of the Holy Spirit, her teen years will be a great time of preparation for adulthood and courageous womanhood. Emphasize your personal commitment to train, guide, and support her through this time. Finally, express your unconditional love for her.

3. Presenting the Letter(s)

At the appropriate time in the ceremony, read your letter aloud to your daughter. A hug or other affirming touch would be very appropriate if your daughter is comfortable with this. Then give the letter to your daughter to keep and treasure always.

Sample Purity Pledge

See next page for a sample purity pledge.

My Heart Belongs to Him

In the sight of God, and through the power of the Holy Spirit, I will strive to maintain moral purity. I will do this by keeping my thoughts pure and by allowing myself to be influenced by the *right things* (the Bible, Christian books, and wholesome television programs, movies, and music) and the *right people* (parents, godly teachers, counselors, and Christian friends).

Finally … whatever is true, whatever is honorable, whatever is right, whatever is pure, whatever is lovely, whatever is of good repute, if there is any excellence and if anything worthy of praise, dwell on these things.

Philippians 4:8

I will strive to maintain emotional purity by keeping my feelings for others pure. I will trust God to guard my heart, which will help keep me from becoming emotionally attached to someone of the opposite sex prematurely—before I'm ready to marry.

And finally, through the power of the Holy Spirit, I will commit to maintain physical purity by abstaining from sexual immorality and by giving Christ first place in every area of my life (Romans 6:13 and Colossians 1:18).

Pledged by:

_____

On:

_____

Witnessed by:

_____

My Heart Belongs to Him — My Identity

Daughter's Guide

Preparing for Courageous Womanhood

Have you ever struggled with self-esteem? Wanting to fit in with the crowd? Knowing how to relate to boys? Ever faced the challenge of making right choices against the strong waves of peer pressure? Wondered how you could challenge your friends to do the right thing without being teased or thought of as not cool?

If you answered yes to any of these questions, this book is for you! *My Heart Belongs to Him* is no ordinary study. It is a unique and exciting journey through God's Word! You will discover who you are in Christ, and what it means when your heart belongs to Him.

My Heart Belongs to Him is designed for you and your mom to work through together! You are sure to grow closer to each other and to God, as you talk and pray about today's tough issues in ways that are comfortable and fun!

This study, *My Identity,* is divided into eight sessions and is filled with stories, real-life situations, activities, projects, and more. You will learn how to strengthen your self-esteem, manage your emotions, guard your purity, make wise choices, and communicate better with family and friends. Discover how making wise choices can help you influence others in a positive way. In addition, you'll gain insights into managing your time, setting goals, and making the most of your life!

This book is not a complete instruction manual for how to live your life. It's more of a guidebook with ways you can navigate the tough issues of teenage life and young womanhood. You'll receive solid direction to set you on the right path as you prepare for courageous womanhood. Become the woman God created you to be—physically, mentally, emotionally, socially, and especially spiritually.

What are you waiting for? Get going! We hope you, like thousands of other young ladies, will learn life skills and values on this journey that will build character into your life and equip you to make a difference in your world for years to come!

Please Read This Before You Begin!

God has a message for you in Jeremiah 29:12-13 that says, " … you will call upon Me and come and pray to Me, and I will listen to you. You will seek Me and find Me, when you search for Me with all your heart." He is really interested in having a close personal relationship with you.

Have you grown up hearing about God all your life, yet never experiencing the abundant, rich relationship He promises? The awesome promises in His Word (the Bible) apply to those who love Jesus and know Him as Savior and Lord. Now may be the time to begin that relationship. If you have never received Christ as your Savior and made Him Lord of your life, check "You Can Know God Personally" in the appendix at the back of the book.

Perhaps you do know Christ, but have neglected your relationship with Him. Now is a great time to turn your heart toward Him as never before and to share your faith with people who may not know Him as Savior and Lord. The appendix can help you share the good news of the gospel. With Mom's (or your leader's) permission, you may even want to invite a friend or two to join you in this study! Remember to keep your friends, especially non-Christian friends, lifted up in prayer. Ask God that they too would come to know Him—His love, His power, His provision, and His guidance.

Get ready for an unforgettable experience that will change your life!

PERSONAL ACTION STEPS

From your Personal Action Steps at the end of each session, select one or two action steps that you want to begin applying. Then write that step(s) on this page, so you can refer to it often.

... because my heart belongs to **Him!**

3

Session 1

Seeing Myself Through God's Eyes

I will give thanks to You,
for I am fearfully and wonderfully made;
Wonderful are Your works,
And my soul knows it very well.

Psalm 139:14

Focus Your worth is not based on your looks, your abilities, where you live, who your friends are, or what others think about you. Instead, your worth is based on how God sees you and values you. When God looks at you, He sees His beautiful, lovable creation, who is full of value and great potential.

You will help your daughter learn to appreciate her value as the person God created her to be as you guide her to:

- Evaluate how she currently sees herself and what factors might be influencing her viewpoint.

- Understand the five general standards that society uses to measure a person's value.

- Learn the dangers of basing self-worth on looks, talents, achievements, or on what others think.

- Understand the dynamics of puberty and how it may affect the way she sees herself.

- Discover how God sees and values her.

- Learn eight practical ways to strengthen her self-worth.

get ready

This section features a fictional story and related discussion questions. It introduces your daughter to the topic and sparks an interest in the material to be covered in this session. Read the story aloud together, then discuss the questions.

THE ACCIDENT

"Mom!" Haley yelled as she slammed the front door behind her.

"I'm in the bedroom!" Her mom yelled back. Haley dropped her backpack in the hallway and raced to the kitchen. "Guess who came back to school today?" she asked as she plopped down at the kitchen table.

"Who, dear?" answered her mom with curiosity.

"Pam! She's finally better, and back to school!"

"Oh, I'm so glad to hear that."

"Yeah, it was good to see her. But she didn't look so good. She's really changed. I feel sorry for her."

"Well, she was in a terrible accident," Mom said. "That car was completely totaled—it's amazing she even survived! I'm sure it will take some time before she gets back to her normal self."

"I guess so … the problem is that people seemed real awkward around her. Some of the kids went up to her to say they were glad she was back, but they didn't know what to say. A lot of kids avoided her and stared at her."

"I thought she was real popular," Haley's mom said.

"She was! Almost all of the girls envied her and wanted to be just like her. And all of the guys had a crush on her. But now, just because she has a scar on her face and walks with a limp, everybody treats her differently. In fact," said Haley hardly taking a breath, "she was sitting all by herself at lunch. I couldn't believe it! Rebecca and I felt so sorry for her that we sat and talked with her so she wouldn't be alone."

"Well, that was a wonderful thing to do. I'm glad you did. How did she say she was doing?"

"Not so good," said Haley with sadness in her voice. "She actually said that she hated herself. She also said that she wished she didn't have to come to school because no one talks to her anymore."

"I'm so sorry to hear that," said her mother looking up from washing dishes. "But you know, Haley, Pam went through quite a bit these last few months. Everything she once valued about herself was gone after the accident. She must be feeling very much alone and unloved."

Haley drifted off into deep thought. She thought about how much value she had placed on her own looks, talents, and abilities. She thought about how good it made her feel to be popular with the kids at school and at church. And she thought about how she might feel if she lost any of those things for any reason.

"I hope that never happens to me," Haley said. "I would never want to feel worthless or walk around like life was not worth living. And I certainly wouldn't want to feel so alone."

let's talk about it

1. How do you think Pam felt about herself before and after the accident? Why do you think her feelings changed?

2. What things were Pam, Haley, and the other kids at school using to measure a person's worth and value?

3. How would you feel about yourself if something happened to change your appearance, intelligence, abilities, or status (position) in a traumatic way? Would you feel like Pam felt? Why or why not?

get real

Everyone has the need to be loved, valued, and understood. And everyone wants to feel that they fit in or belong. When these needs are met in your life, you will probably feel good about yourself.

How you feel about yourself influences everything about you, including how well you do in school, the type of friends you choose, the type of activities you get involved in, and many other choices you make. If your "self-esteem" is too high or too low, you will feel insecure about yourself and how you relate to others. And as you go through your teenage years, insecurity can keep you from becoming all that God wants you to be.

HOW SELF-WORTH IS SHAPED

The way you feel about yourself is shaped by many different factors in your life. Your parents are probably the biggest influence. For example, if your parents constantly criticize you, you will probably grow up feeling insecure or even worthless. Or you might do anything you can to win the approval of others because your parents never gave you that approval. On the other hand, if your parents work hard to encourage you and love you, you will probably grow up feeling good about yourself.

Many teenagers base their self-worth on what their friends or classmates think about them. They try hard to say and do the right things and wear the right clothes so that others will think they are cool. Some base their self-worth on their looks, talents, or achievements—like how well they do in school, or perform in a sport, or sing, or dance, or draw. Others base their self-worth on their relationship with God and on how He feels about them. They feel good about themselves because they know how much He loves and values them.

let's talk about it

1. Why is having healthy self-esteem so important?
    Suggested answer: When you have healthy self-esteem you feel good about yourself and your strengths, and at the same time you recognize and accept your weaknesses. You place value on who you are and what you have to offer, rather than being jealous of another person's looks, abilities, or position in life. You are happy to be you, just the way God created you, but you realize your need to grow and strive to become all

8

that God wants you to be. Feeling good about yourself gives you the courage to use your God-given gifts, talents, and abilities to serve Him and to help others.

2. What do you think are the dangers of basing your self-worth on what other people think about you?

3. What do you think are the dangers of basing your self-worth on your own looks, talents, or achievements?

How Society Measures a Person's Value

Society uses five main standards to determine a person's worth or value. They are appearance or physical beauty, intelligence, talent, status, and wealth.

- People who are thought of as attractive or smart are treated better and valued more than those who are not.
- Those considered intelligent get more attention and opportunities.
- If you are talented, good at sports, music, the arts, speech, and so on, you will be recognized and respected by others for your talent.
- Society will also determine your worth or value based on how much money you have, which is measured by where you live, who your parents are, and what they do for a living.
- And if you hold a high position, such as captain of the cheerleaders or class president, you will be valued and respected by others.

Any time you trust these standards for your self-worth ... watch out! Think about it. It's impossible to measure up in all of these five areas. You might do great in class, but you're not so good in sports. Or you may be the best basketball player on the team, but someone makes fun of you because you don't do well in math. You might be the smartest student in your school, but you're constantly teased because you live in a poor neighborhood. Or you might think your looks are great until you pick up some teen magazine and see a skinny model and think you need to lose weight.

let's talk about it

1. How can basing your self-worth on society's standards hurt you? Suggested answer: Evaluating yourself by the standards society uses can cause your self-esteem to be either too high or too low. It all depends on how you feel you measure up. The truth is no one can ever measure up to everyone's expectations all of the time. And when you do not measure up, you may begin to feel worthless and unloved, which can lead to emotional struggles like stress and anxiety, self-pity, discouragement, fear, or a lack of confidence. You can become overly sensitive, critical of others, and can develop a habit of comparing yourself with others.

2. Do you think it is possible to still feel worthless or unhappy if you are attractive, intelligent, talented, or wealthy? Why or why not? Suggested answer: Yes, because those things cannot guarantee happiness or fill the emptiness in a person's heart. You always feel you are in competition with other people. It is extremely difficult to stay on top, and circumstances can change at any time—you can't assume you will always be wealthy and intelligent and talented.

3. What standards do your peers use to measure a person's value? What standards do you use? What happens when a person doesn't measure up to those standards? Are they excluded from the "in crowd," thought of as a nerd, or worse? Should peers try to measure up to each other's standards? Why or why not?

LOOKING FOR LOVE

Have you ever said anything like the following? "I hate the way I look … " "I can't do anything right … " "Nobody likes me … " "I wish I were more like … "

When people are down on themselves, there is a feeling of emptiness inside their hearts that they will try desperately to fill. Unfortunately, many people try to find love and acceptance by changing things about themselves—their friends, their appearance, or even their moral choices. Teenage girls who have a low sense of self-worth may look for love in a relationship with a boy. Or they may turn to unhealthy dieting to feel good about themselves. Others might start drinking alcohol or taking drugs to fit in with the crowd. No matter how hard you try to find the love you're looking for, you will always feel insecure when you look in the wrong places.

Sometimes a person's sense of self-worth is too high because their looks, talents, or achievements earn them the love and attention of other people. They may not realize it, but they, too, are seeking love and acceptance in the wrong way. They are basing their self-worth on things that are not secure, that can change at any time.

People with low self-esteem often exhibit these symptoms:

- negative outlook on life, extremely shy and withdrawn
- inability to control anger
- tendency to hide true feelings
- over-emphasis on pleasing others
- tendency to overload on activities
- tendency to be a follower instead of a leader
- tendency toward bad habits and behaviors
- tendency to talk down about themselves
- continually striving to be like someone else
- low achievement in school
- lack of motivation
- isolation
- strained relationships
- low standards and morals
- tendency to shift blame to others for their own mistakes
- … and so on.

let's talk about it

1. Do you know anyone who is looking for love and acceptance in the wrong way? How can you tell?

2. Besides those things previously listed, what are some other things a person might do to find love, acceptance, and self-worth?
Suggested answer: They might over-commit themselves to other people, events, or activities to gain the love and approval of others. They may try to change who they really are to become the type of person they think others will like. They may make wrong choices just to impress others—such as stealing, being disrespectful to adults, or skipping classes.

3. Does having good self-esteem mean that you are conceited?
Suggested answer: No. Having good self-esteem doesn't mean that you are conceited. Rather it means that you have a healthy sense of self-respect. You don't have to worry about what others think about you. You already know your own value. And because of this, you can give yourself away (your love, time, and talents) by helping to build up others, rather than becoming preoccupied with yourself and trying to please people.

4. Do you know anyone who is thought of as conceited? How do you think people would treat this person if something were to happen to change his/her appearance, intelligence, abilities, or status (position) in a dramatic way? How do you think that he/she would feel?

SELF-ESTEEM CHECK!

Take a few minutes to complete this personal evaluation to discover how you feel about yourself in the following areas. Rate each statement on the following scale:

5: strongly agree
4: agree
3: don't know
2: disagree
1: strongly disagree

I am pleased with ...

_____a. My height and weight

_____b. My complexion

_____c. My facial features (eyes, ears, nose, lips, and teeth)

_____d. My hair

_____e. My shape (breasts, hips, legs, feet, etc.)

_____f. My grades and ability to achieve in school

_____g. My athletic ability and/or performance on spirit teams

_____h. My artistic abilities (musical, dancing, drawing, creativity, and hobbies)

_____i. My ability to make friends

_____j. My overall personality

_____k. My parents' acceptance of me (approval of who I am, what I do, and the friends I choose)

_____l. My parents' discipline (moral standards they set, strictness, leniency, and freedom they give me)

_____m. My parents' affection toward me (love shown, how we get along, etc.)

_____n. My parents' love toward each other

_____o. My parents' intelligence and level of success

_____p. My race or nationality

_____q. My home

_____r. My neighborhood

_____s. My friends (the type of friends I have, their acceptance of me, our activities, etc.)

_____t. My church and my spiritual development

TOTAL SCORE _____

Based on this survey ...

- If your score is 80-100, you are very pleased with yourself in these areas.

- If your score is 70-79, you are fairly pleased with yourself in these areas.

- A score of 60 or below may mean you have some concerns about how you measure up in these areas.

If you are the parent of a girl who rates her relationship with her parents low, you will really need to focus on making improvements. Listen carefully to your daughter and remain calm. Seek counseling for your family if there are significant issues. If you are leading a girl through this study who is not your daughter, and you find issues with parents, gently approach the parents after talking with the girl. Explain what you see and offer some helps. If you suspect abuse, you must contact your pastor and the legal authorities to investigate. You need to act on the girl's behalf.

let's talk about it

1. According to the results of your personal evaluation, would you say that you feel good about yourself? Would you say that your view of your self-worth is healthy—or is it too low or too high?

2.. What are some of your main areas of concern? Why?

Tip:

You may want to give your daughter some guidance on what things she can or cannot change and help her understand why. Discuss a plan for those things that can be changed to help strengthen her self-image.

3. Are any of the areas of concern things that you can change? If so, what would you change and how could you make those changes in a healthy way?

let's pray about it

Ask God to help you learn how to appreciate your value as the person He created you to be, and to learn how to see yourself through His eyes, not through the eyes of other people or through the standards set by society. Ask Him to help you change the things that you can to strengthen your self-esteem, and to accept those things that you cannot change.

STOP HERE! If you prefer to do this session in two parts, you may find this to be a natural place to stop. However, if you want to complete this session in one sitting, please continue.

get direction

The first step toward building healthy self-esteem is to fill any emptiness in your heart with God and His love for you. His love is secure. It never changes (see Romans 8:38-39). It is not based on how you look, how popular you are, or even on how well you can perform at one thing or another. His love is unconditional. He won't ever put you down, criticize you, tease you, or laugh at you when you make a mistake. When God looks at you, He sees His beautiful, lovable creation!

God created you as a unique and special person for a divine purpose. There are some things about you that you can change, and God wants you to grow in those areas. But there are also some things about you that you cannot change. And those are the things that God wants you to accept and to use for His glory. He wants to use you to make a positive difference in the lives of those around you, and to draw other people to Himself through the influence of your life. He has given you specific gifts, talents, and abilities for that purpose.

As you draw closer and closer to Him, you will discover that your worth and value are not based on your looks, your abilities, where you live, who your friends are, or even on what guys are noticing you. The truth of the matter is that your worth and value are solely based on your relationship with Christ. When you learn to see yourself through His eyes, feeling good about yourself is so much easier. That's when you can say as the psalmist wrote in Psalm 139:14a, "I will give thanks to You, for I am fearfully and wonderfully made."

This section provides a clear picture of what the Bible has to say about this topic. The biblical truths and principles examined in this section will help your daughter apply God's Word to her life.

let's talk about it

1. Look up the following Scriptures and write what each has to say about how you—a child of God—measure up in God's eyes.

Appearance: Psalm 139:13-15
Suggested answer: God skillfully created you in your mother's womb like a precious work of art.

Intelligence: 1 Corinthians 2:16

Suggested answer: When you trust and accept Jesus as your Savior and Lord, God gives you the mind of Christ. As you draw closer to Him and learn of Him, you will begin to think like Him more and more—think the kinds of thoughts that He would have, considering what He would say, and what He would do in everyday situations.

Talents: 1 Corinthians 12:4-11, 28

Suggested answer: God gives His people different gifts for different purposes, primarily to show His power at work in our lives, to help others, and to build His Kingdom. For example, to some He gives the ability to give wise advice, while others may be especially good at studying and teaching.

Status: 1 Peter 2:9

Suggested answer: You are royalty! You have been chosen by God Himself and are His very own.

Wealth: Galatians 4:7

Suggested answer: As Christians, we are all given the full rights of being a son of God; and as His children, we are also His heirs.

2. How do you feel about the way God views you in the five areas that the world uses to measure a person's value? How can knowing how God feels about you change the way you feel about yourself?

Suggested answer: Knowing how valuable you are to God can change your whole outlook on how you view yourself. This knowledge makes feeling good about yourself so much easier and can help you to achieve and succeed at becoming all that God created you to be, in spite of what anyone else may think or say about you.

3. What would you say are some of your strengths? What would you say are your God-given gifts or talents? For example, you may be good at singing, dancing, drawing, playing a sport, organizing, leading, teaching, or helping others. What are some ways that you can use your strengths, gifts, and talents to serve God and to help others?

THE GIRL IN THE MIRROR

You might be thinking, *But when I look in the mirror, I don't like what I see. I don't have the figure that I want, I can't get my hair to do what I want it to do, and I have zits!*

Right now you are going through a time in your life known as puberty—or if you haven't started yet, you will soon! It's a time when your body goes through a lot of changes. You may notice your body developing and maturing into the shape of a woman. You might feel like it's all happening too soon, or maybe not soon enough.

Your menstrual cycle may begin, which can be exciting and scary at the same time. And you may have already discovered that with menstruation comes a host of emotional ups and downs, and maybe some physical discomfort, like cramping. And, yes, your face may even break out in pimples from time to time. Many changes are taking place as you grow and mature. And in the midst of all of these changes, you may start to notice guys, who may have also begun noticing you.

Everyone has to go through puberty. You can easily begin to criticize yourself during this time. And because your peers are going through the same thing, they can also be pretty critical. The teasing can be even more intense than when you were younger. Just remember that, for the most part, they too are struggling with changes and insecurities. You may want to remind them that no one is perfect; therefore, no one should tease. Teasing is wrong and it hurts.

If you've got the puberty blues, take heart! The good news is that puberty is just for a season. This too will pass! So the next time someone teases you, just remember that it's not what others think or say about you that really counts. In God's eyes, you are a person of great worth and value! No matter what anyone thinks, and no matter what anyone says, always remember that the God of all creation loves you and thinks you are special! What an honor … what a blessing!

let's talk about it

1. What are some of the changes you are seeing in your life and body as a result of puberty? How do you feel about those changes?

2. Do friends tease you? If so, how does their teasing make you feel?

3. QUESTIONS TO ASK MOM:

    a. What was it like for you when you experienced puberty?

    b. Did you have any struggles?

    c. Were you teased?

My Heart Belongs to Him — My Identity

get going

EIGHT WAYS TO STRENGTHEN YOUR SELF-WORTH

1. Grow in your relationship with Christ. Spend time with Him and spend time in His Word. This will help you see yourself as a valuable part of God's creation and celebrate the unique, gifted person He created you to be.

2. Don't compare yourself with others, put yourself down, or dwell on your weaknesses. Instead, develop your strengths. Avoid giving yourself negative labels ("I am ugly," "I am good for nothing," and so on). Remember, the Bible says in Proverbs 23:7a, "For as he thinks within himself, so he is." We tend to become the labels we give ourselves.

3. See your mistakes as opportunities to learn, grow, and improve. When you sin, admit it to God, ask for His forgiveness, and refuse to condemn yourself (Romans 8:1). God forgives your sin, and then remembers your sin no more. His love for you never changes (1 John 1:9).

4. Graciously accept compliments and praise, and learn to compliment and encourage others (1 Thessalonians 5:11).

5. Choose the right kinds of friends—those who will build you up, support you, and love you for who you are (1 Corinthians 15:33).

6. Take good care of yourself and learn to enjoy life (John 10:10)! Get healthy rest, maintain a healthy diet, exercise, and find activities that you really enjoy. Treat yourself from time to time. You're the apple of God's eye (Zecharaiah 2:8)!

7. Strive to look your personal best with neatly groomed hair, nails, clothing, etc. (1 Timothy 2:9-10).

8. Turn your focus toward serving God rather than yourself (Matthew 22:36-39).

This is the life application section of the session. It includes practical guidelines and action points to help your daughter live out what she has learned.

IMPORTANT NOTE:

If your daughter has not invited Christ into her life, walk her through "You Can Know God Personally" in the appendix.

Don't pressure her to make a decision. Share openly with her and allow God to draw her in His time. If she is not ready to respond, just continue through the study and ask God to touch her heart.

let's pray about it

Thank God for creating you as the unique and special person that you are. Then ask Him to help you accept yourself for who you are. Build on your God-given strengths, gifts, talents, and abilities, so that you can positively influence others and bring Him glory.

Here's what I discovered in this session:

POINT OF DISCOVERY

Here your daughter will record the key principles that she has learned in this session (those truths that stood out to her the most). If your daughter needs help, feel free to offer suggestions.

Because my heart belongs to Him I will:

PERSONAL ACTION STEPS

Your daughter will record the personal changes she plans to make in her life as a result of what she has learned. Again, feel free to offer suggestions if she needs help.

NOTE: Have your daughter select one or two action points that she most wants to apply, and then have her write it (them) on the Personal Action Steps sheet on page 3 of her book.

keep moving

This section features additional projects. They are designed to help your daughter deepen her experience, and to encourage you to participate in her growth process. Feel free to use one or more of the assignments or projects presented, or use your creativity to create one or two of your own.

Therefore if anyone is in Christ, he is a new creature; the old things passed away; behold new things have come.

2 Corinthians 5:17

Over the next week or so, try the following:

A. Practice counteracting negative thoughts with positive thoughts, such as promises from God's Word. For example, if you are thinking, *I hate the way I look,* you can recite Psalm 139:14, "… I am fearfully and wonderfully made … ." If you are thinking, *I can't do anything right,* or feel as though there is something you can't do because you're afraid you might fail, you can recite Philippians 4:13, "I can do all things through Him who strengthens me." [1]

B. Read 2 Corinthians 5:17. When you receive Christ, you become brand new. You could say we're like butterflies. Don't you think butterflies are awesome? Just think about it. At one time a butterfly was a caterpillar, resembling an ugly worm that crawls on the ground. Then, after going through a rebirth process in the cocoon, it became a beautiful new creature!

That's how it is with people. No matter how attractive we might look, or how good we are at sports, or how valuable we may be to other people, before we give our hearts to Christ we are really no better than the ugly worm, because of our sin. But the very moment you give your heart to Jesus and trust Him to be your Savior and Lord you become a new creature! Like the butterfly, you are born again! And because your heart belongs to Him, He loves you and accepts you just as you are, right now … today!

C. The following Scriptures are proof of God's love for you. These are just a few of many. See how many other Scriptures you can find that tell of God's love for you. [2]

He sacrificed for you:
> *For God so loved the world, that He gave His only begotten Son, that whoever believes in Him shall not perish, but have eternal life.*
>
> John 3:16

He chose you:
> *Long ago, even before he made the world, God chose us to be his very own, through what Christ would do for us; he decided then to make us*

holy in his eyes, without a single fault—we who stand before him covered with his love. His unchanging plan has always been to adopt us into his own family by sending Jesus Christ to die for us. And he did this because he wanted to!

Ephesians 1:4,5 TLB

He has a plan for your life:

"For I know the plans I have for you," says the Lord. "They are plans for good and not for evil, to give you a future and a hope."

Jeremiah 29:11 TLB

He wants to meet your needs:

Since He did not spare even his own Son for us but gave Him up for us all, won't He also surely give us everything else?

Romans 8:32 TLB

He wants to carry your burdens and help you:

Give your burdens to the Lord. He will carry them.

Psalm 55:22a TLB

He promises to never leave you:

He Himself has said, "I will never desert you, nor will I ever forsake you."

Hebrews 13:5b

He thinks of you constantly:

How precious it is, Lord, to realize that you are thinking about me constantly! I can't even count how many times a day your thoughts turn towards me. And when I waken in the morning, you are still thinking of me!

Psalm 139:17,18 TLB

Session 2

Radiating True Beauty Inside and Out

*Don't let the world around you
squeeze you into its mold,
but let God remake you so that
your whole attitude of mind is changed.*

Romans 12:2 (Phillips translation)

Reflection

To review the previous session and to follow up on projects and assignments, ask your daughter the following four questions:

1. Thinking back over the previous session, what life-changing truth would you say stood out most to you?

2. How are you doing on your "Personal Action Steps" from the last session?

3. What progress have you made with your "Keep Moving" assignments and/or projects from the previous session? (Be sure to encourage her to complete those assignments or projects that she has not yet completed.)

4. Is there anything else from the previous session that you would like to talk about?

Focus

True beauty comes from within your heart as a result of knowing Christ as Savior and Lord. It can be seen when you allow His love to shine through you from the inside out. It shows in your attitude, your words, and your actions, and it's reflected when you make right choices in your everyday life. This kind of beauty is far more important, according to God's Word, than the shallow beauty of a shapely body, a pretty face, and fashionable clothing.

OBJECTIVES:

You will help your daughter discover the beauty that God created in her as you guide her to:

- Understand society's standard of beauty and the dangers of pursuing that standard.

- Evaluate her idea of beauty and how passionate she may be about achieving that image.

- Explore the Scriptures to discover God's standard of beauty.

- Understand that God desires our focus to be His standard of beauty, not the world's standard of beauty.

- Understand that God created her with special features and characteristics that make her uniquely beautiful.

- Learn how to radiate true beauty inside and out.

get ready

This section features a fictional story and related discussion questions. It introduces your daughter to the topic and sparks an interest in the material to be covered in this session. Read the story aloud together, then discuss the questions.

WHEN BEAUTY IS THE BEAST

While at Shelly's house for a sleepover, Haley, Rebecca, and a couple of other girls from school started talking about size and weight as they browsed through several teen magazines. Shelly's mom overheard some of their conversation when she walked through the room where the girls were talking.

After pointing out which models in the magazines they wanted to look like, the girls began to discuss their individual plans to get their bodies down to the "perfect size."

"I'm going on a diet," said Marianne.

"Oh, I heard diets don't work," said Haley, "I'm going to work out every day!"

"I'm going to do both," said Rebecca. "My mom says I need to eat right and get regular exercise."

"Well, I'm bigger than all of you," said Amy. "I'm not going to let you walk around looking like models while I look like a pig."

Shelly just sat quietly, and then quickly changed the subject.

Now Shelly's mom understood why her daughter was barely eating. Every time it was the same excuse: "I'm not hungry."

Shelly's mom went straight to a phone in the back of the house and called her friend Janet. When they were teenagers, Janet became obsessed with losing weight and began to starve herself. Before long she had an eating disorder called anorexia. Now, years later, Janet's life was dedicated to helping young girls with eating disorders.

Janet agreed to come right over to talk with Shelly and her friends. During her visit, she showed the girls pictures of real teenagers who had starved themselves to lose weight. She explained eating disorders and their effects on the body. She told real-life stories of girls who had suffered with anorexia and bulimia and about those who had even died. Then she shared about her own fight with anorexia, as a teenager, and how she still suffers from its side effects.

"You see, girls, when we become obsessed with society's standard of beauty," said Janet, "beauty can become a beast … one that is sometimes very, very difficult to slay."

The next day, after all of her friends had gone home, Shelly and her mother sat down to talk about Janet's visit. As Shelly began to share, tears welled up in her eyes. She talked about how she had grown to hate her body and how much she wanted to be skinny like other girls. Then Shelly confided in her mother that she was in trouble. She admitted that she, too, like some of the girls Janet shared about, had lost control over her desire to lose weight.

let's talk about it

1. What do you think about the ways the girls wanted to fulfill their ideas of beauty?

2. What do you think might have happened to Shelly if her mom (1) had not noticed the change in her eating habits and (2) had not acted right away to get some help?

3. Do you find yourself having the desire to become "beautiful" in unhealthy ways? Explain.

get real

This section gives an overview of the topic. It gives your daughter "the big picture" as it is in our world today; for example "this is what's happening out there—this is what young women are facing." It will help your daughter relate to the topic on a personal level.

Our world's idea of beauty for women is the "fashion model figure," which few women could have unless they practically starved themselves. Beauty is seen as so important in our society that we have beauty contests for men, women, and children of all ages. Every year, billions of dollars are spent on advertisements on television and in magazines to promote things that we can buy or do to make ourselves more beautiful. There are contact lenses to change your eye color, hair dyes to change your hair color, makeup to enhance your facial features, fitness centers and programs to help trim off excess body fat, and surgeries to change the way you look!

You may have noticed that even at school the more attractive kids are often the most popular. And how many girls do you know who are interested in a guy because of his looks, without really knowing anything about his character or personality? Later on in life, a person's appearance plays a part in their getting a job, finding a husband or wife, choosing friends, and so on. Many people think that they can't succeed at anything unless they look right.

let's talk about it

1. What is your idea of beauty? How do you think a girl needs to look in order to be seen as beautiful?

2. What are your friends' ideas of beauty?

Tip:

For fun, look through some magazines together and point out how many advertisements promote things that we can do or buy to make ourselves more beautiful. As you go through the magazines, you might want to point out the sizes and shapes of the models. Which models look healthy? Which models look dangerously thin? Which models does your daughter find attractive? Why?

3. What kinds of things are you and your friends doing to fulfill your idea of beauty?

THE DANGERS OF PURSUING THE WORLD'S STANDARD OF BEAUTY

Because of the pressure put on women to look like today's fashion models, more and more teenage girls are becoming obsessed with losing weight. Many of them are so determined to become "skinny" that they even sacrifice their health to reach their goals. In addition to over-exercising or trying diet pills, some girls develop eating disorders. Anorexia is a disorder where people starve themselves. Those with bulimia overeat on purpose (or "binge"), and then they empty themselves (or "purge") after eating—usually by vomiting. An eating disorder can cause serious health problems such as a weakened heart, constipation, dry and brittle skin, hair loss, and even death.

Girls with eating disorders often end up losing control of their own actions and of their understanding of reality. For example, a 16-year-old girl weighing only 60 pounds may still think she is not thin enough. She refuses to eat more than three tablespoons of cottage cheese per day or a small plateful of lettuce a couple of times per day. Even though she is dangerously thin and her health is failing, she can't stop herself. In her case, medical help, hospitalization, counseling, and support from family and friends will all be needed to help her stop the cycle and save her life.

Are you obsessed with dieting and losing weight in an effort to look like a fashion model? Complete the following survey adapted from *Beauty and the Best*, by Debra L. Evans, to determine how important beauty is to you. Choose the answer for each question that comes closest to your experience. (If more than one answer applies, choose the answer with the highest number of points.) After you have completed the survey, check your total. Then ask yourself, "How passionate am I about achieving society's idea of beauty?"

Tip:
You may want to do some research on this in advance and find a magazine article or a book that tells the real-life story of someone who has struggled with either of these eating disorders. It would be great if you could find one with pictures. A real-life story always has a greater impact than fiction or even factual information. This may help your daughter understand further the seriousness of these disorders.

Are You a Beauty Junkie? [1]

Answer the following questions:

a. I've dieted to lose weight during the last

___ 24 hours (10 points)

___ month (5 points)

___ year (1 point)

___ decade (0 points)

b. I look at other (young) women's appearances and compare myself to them

___ almost always (10 points)

___ frequently (5 points)

___ rarely (1 point)

___ never (0 points)

c. I normally weigh myself

___ more than once a day (10 points)

___ daily (5 points)

___ several times a week (3 points)

___ weekly (2 points)

___ monthly (1 point)

___ annually or only at medical check-ups (0 points)

d. When I'm in public without any makeup on, I feel

___ ugly (10 points)

___ naked, invisible, or below potential (5 points)

___ plain (1 point)

___ no differently than if I am wearing makeup (0 points)

e. I worry about my weight or my appearance

___ once an hour or more (10 points)

___ off and on throughout the day (5 points)

___ a few times a week (1 point)

___ hardly ever (0 points)

My Heart Belongs to Him — My Identity

f. Almost every time I eat, at least once, I usually think about

___ how much I should weigh or how fat I am (10 points)

___ the number of fat grams/calories I'm consuming (5 points)

___ ways to satisfy my hunger appropriately (1 point)

___ enjoying and being thankful for my meal (0 points)

g. When I look in the mirror, I typically see

___ every imperfection (10 points)

___ several imperfections (5 points)

___ a few imperfections (1 point)

___ myself (0 points)

TOTAL SCORE _____

Tip:
Discuss with your daughter the results of the survey. In which areas did she score the highest? Why? Discuss with her how passionate she may be about achieving society's standard of beauty. What signs have you noticed? This is an area that many young women really struggle with. Be prayerful about your daughter's responses and determine whether or not there may be a need for counseling or professional assistance to overcome any area she may be personally struggling with.

- If you scored more than 50 points, you are very pre-occupied with beauty issues. It is likely that our world's ideas and expectations about beauty greatly influence the way you see yourself—as well as the way you see others.

- If you scored 21-49 points, it's likely that the world's standard of beauty influences you in a number of ways, but is not all-consuming.

- If you scored 5-20 points, the world's standard of beauty has very little influence in your life.

- If you scored less than five points, you either haven't reached the stage in your life where you give much thought to beauty, or you live on another planet, where there are no beauty advertisements.

let's pray about it

Talk to God and ask Him to show you what it really means to be beautiful and to help you change your focus from the world's idea of beauty to His idea of beauty. Ask Him to help you discover, through His Word and through this session, the beauty He created in you.

STOP HERE! If you prefer to do this session in two parts, you may find this to be a natural place to stop. However, if you want to complete this session in one sitting, please continue.

get direction

God created each and every woman special. We are like one huge flower garden. All the flowers are beautiful, and yet flowers come in many shapes, colors, and sizes. God is very creative! Every woman, young and old, is uniquely beautiful—each with her own God-given features and characteristics. Why would an orchid want to become a rose anyway? Both are uniquely beautiful. Trying to measure up to the images you see on television or in a magazine can teach you to hate your own body and can give you the wrong idea of real beauty.

REAL BEAUTY ISN'T SKIN DEEP!

Real beauty cannot be found by trying to clone a fashion model; neither can it be found by trying to look just like your peers or your favorite teen idol. It is not having the perfect features and the perfect figure as shown on television, or in movies and magazines. Real beauty isn't skin deep. It goes much deeper than what you can see on the outside.

The Bible teaches that real beauty comes from within. And it begins when you give your heart and life to Christ and allow His love to shine through you. It shows when you handle conflict with fairness—admitting your faults and forgiving others when they make mistakes. And real beauty is reflected when you make right choices in your everyday life. This kind of beauty is far more important, according to God's Word, than the shallow beauty that a shapely body, a pretty face, and fashionable clothing can give.

When real beauty shines from your heart and life, other people will be drawn to you like a magnet. Those around you will want to know what makes you different and what makes you so attractive. Then you can tell them about God's love and the difference He makes in your life. That's what real beauty is all about.

let's talk about it

1. Have you ever met or known anyone who was beautiful on the outside but had a rotten personality? How did her personality affect the way people saw her?

2. Have you ever met or known anyone who was considered to be unattractive on the outside but had a warm, fun-loving personality? How did her personality affect the way people saw her?

3. What are you more known for, your inner beauty or your outer beauty? Which is really more important?

4. The Bible teaches that inner beauty helps us reflect Christ to the world. What do the following Scriptures say that we, as representatives of Christ, are to be to the world?

   a. 1 Timothy 4:12

   Suggested answer: We are to be an example to the world of those who are followers of Christ in the way we talk, act, love, exercise faith, and live.

   b. Matthew 5:14-16

   Suggested answer: We are to be a light to the world by making wise choices so that people will see our good works and give praise to God as a result.

Tip:
To explain further why inner beauty is more important than outer beauty, you can share with your daughter that she could be the most beautifully dressed young lady at her school, with the most stylish haircut and well-groomed nails, but if she does not act like a beautiful young lady, her beauty will not be noticed or fully appreciated. Our actions speak loud and clear, and sometimes our actions—when they are unattractive—can drown out the loveliest appearance. It is, therefore, extremely important that we carry ourselves with love, dignity, and respect at all times.

c. 1 Peter 2:9

Suggested answer: We are to let our lives be examples of how God can change a person's life, showing how He called us out of darkness (evil, wrong choices) into His wonderful light (godly living, right choices).

WHAT ABOUT PHYSICAL BEAUTY?

Therefore we are ambassadors for Christ, as though God were making an appeal through us; we beg you on behalf of Christ, be reconciled to God.

2 Corinthians 5:20

God does not say to do away with all concern for physical beauty; He just doesn't want it to be your main concern. He wants you to know that He loves you with an everlasting love and that no amount of dieting, exercise, makeup, plastic surgery, or changes in hair and eye color will cause God to love you any more or any less.

However, we do live in a world where people make judgments about you according to the messages you send with your outward appearance. The clothes you wear, how you style your hair, how you wear your make-up, and how you carry yourself in public give people clues about who you are and what you are like on the inside. All of those things help to shape your reputation. And everything that you do should reflect Christ, because as a Christian, you represent Him to the world (see 2 Corinthians 5:20).

 let's talk about it

1. What can you learn about God's idea of beauty from the following Scriptures?

a. 1 Samuel 16:7

Suggested answer: What's important to God is the condition of your heart, not your outward appearance.

b. 1 Peter 3:3-4

Suggested answer: Outer beauty should not be our focus. Godly character that originates in the heart is precious in the sight of God. In His eyes, that is true beauty.

c. Proverbs 31:30

Suggested answer: Charm can be deceiving, and outer beauty doesn't last, neither does it have any eternal benefits. But a woman who fears and respects the Lord is the one who will be praised.

d. Colossians 3:12-14

Suggested answer: The clothing you wear should not be external only. Every day you should also clothe yourself with the spiritual garments of love, compassion, humility, kindness, gentleness, and patience. This type of clothing radiates beauty in your actions, not just your appearance like regular clothing.

2. Look at the following examples and write down what message each person seems to send with his or her outward appearance.

a. A teenage girl at school who wears a lot of make-up on her face, low-cut blouses, tightly fitted jeans or mini-skirts, and high heels:

Suggested answer: She appears to be seductive—giving an open invitation for guys to pursue her for the purpose of sex.

b. A guy at your school that dyes his hair in different colors and wears nothing but black:

Suggested answer: He appears to like drawing attention to himself. Black may communicate he is part of a gang or cult. He seems to be sending a message of darkness and evil. He may be preoccupied with death.

c. A young woman wearing a neatly pressed, becoming dress of modest length, an attractive haircut, and a small amount of makeup:

Suggested answer: She communicates modesty. She seems to be concerned about setting a godly example, drawing more attention to her values than to her looks.

3. Think of some of the current styles of clothing today—what are the kids at your school wearing? What styles or fashion trends do you think God may want you to avoid? Why?

Suggested answer: Avoid things like crop tops, tightly fitted jeans or pants, short shorts, short dresses and skirts, low necklines, tight shirts, and see-through material. These things communicate that you are trying to look and be seductive, which is inappropriate.

get going

This is the life application section of the session. It includes practical guidelines and action points to help your daughter live out what she has learned.

God wants you to know that He loves you and that He accepts and appreciates you as you are. However, He does want you to grow. Therefore, whether you are cutting calories, exercising, sharpening a talent or skill, or making any other changes to improve yourself, remember to first look to Him for direction, and trust Him to guide you to do what is right. "Trust in the Lord with all your heart, and do not lean on your own understanding. In all your ways acknowledge Him, and He will make your paths straight" (Proverbs 3:5-6).

DRESS TO IMPRESS

Don't dress to draw attention to your outward appearance. Instead, make a positive impression on others with your inner beauty and godly values. And remember, the clothes you wear on the outside creatively express who you are on the inside.

Most teenage girls feel more at ease when they dress like their friends. That is not all bad; just keep two things in mind when you shop:

- 🍂 First, make sure you don't trade in your moral values (modesty) just to model the latest styles. It is possible to dress fashionably with modesty (see 1 Timothy 2:9,10).

- 🍂 Second, don't lose your own identity. Use your imagination. Be genuine, not an imitation. Dare to be yourself! If you are brave enough to be yourself by dressing to reflect your own individuality and personal values, people will admire you for it.

Likewise, I want women to adorn themselves with proper clothing, modestly and discreetly, not with braided hair and gold or pearls or costly garments, but rather by means of good works, as is proper for women making a claim to godliness.

1 Timothy 2:9-10

My Heart Belongs to Him — My Identity

TAKE CARE OF YOUR BODY

To function at its best, your body needs the right kind of fuel (a healthy variety of foods), proper rest, and regular exercise. Try to eat three healthy and balanced meals every day, with healthy snacks (fruits, nuts, raw veggies, etc.) between meals. Make sure you exercise at least three times a week. Aerobic exercise is best—swimming, cycling, jogging, walking, and so on (be sure to consult your doctor before starting any exercise program, and to start out slowly). Also, try to get enough sleep every night to allow your body to rest and recharge. Pay close attention to personal hygiene. And always remember to avoid activities that would be harmful to your body and mind such as drinking, smoking, and using drugs.

Tip:
Suggest that your daughter develop a fitness program that she and a friend can do together on a regular basis, such as brisk walking, jogging, aerobics, or swimming. You may even want to suggest that the two of you do a fitness program together. Whatever she chooses to do, she should make it fun and be faithful!

let's talk about it

1. What is involved in maintaining good personal hygiene?

Suggested answer: Personal hygiene involves bathing regularly, keeping your fingernails and toenails neatly trimmed and clean, using underarm deodorant faithfully every day to counteract natural perspiration, regularly brushing your teeth, using a mouthwash, flossing, and using breath fresheners throughout the day, as necessary.

Additional ideas: Also, make sure that your clothes are clean, properly laundered, and pressed. Make sure your shoes are not scuffed, worn down, or dingy. Never wear pantyhose with visible runs, and repair all holes, missing buttons, or broken zippers before wearing an outfit. Check to see that your slip does not hang past your dress or skirt hemline, and make sure you have no visible panty-lines, or bra or lingerie straps.

2. Would you say that you're doing a good job with personal hygiene, or could you use some improvement? Explain.

Or do you not know that your body is a temple of the Holy Spirit who is in you, whom you have from God, and that you are not your own?

1 Corinthians 6:19

MAKE THE BEST OF WHO YOU ARE

We each have what we (not God) would consider imperfections—a large nose, narrow eyes, thin hair, etc. Perhaps what you consider an imperfection may be what makes you unique. Appreciate your uniqueness … God created you that way. Take pride in the real you. If you think you are beautiful and carry yourself in a graceful way (radiating beauty inside and out), others will think you are beautiful, too.

And remember being truly beautiful on the outside is the result of being beautiful on the inside. When you send the right message with your outward appearance, make sure that the content of that message is in place on the inside. Imagine someone giving you a beautifully wrapped box. But when you open it, there's dirty laundry inside. The message the beautifully wrapped box sent is deceitful—it led you to believe something that was not really there.

Be as beautiful on the inside as you are on the outside, so that you are sending an honest message. Let confidence, friendliness, love, joy, a servant's heart, and other godly characteristics fill your heart and shine in your life, so that you are presenting a total package. Then, when others see you, they will see Jesus, and they'll want to know more about Him as a result of your life. That is true beauty!

let's talk about it

1. What messages could you be sending with your outward appearance?

2. Are you sending the same messages with your inward appearance? Explain.

3. Are changes needed? If so, what are some practical ways to make those changes?

Talk to God about helping you accept and appreciate the way He made you. Ask Him to give you the wisdom, strength, and courage to make whatever changes may be necessary so that you can present to the world your personal best—inside and out.

Here your daughter will record the key principles that she has learned in this session (those truths that stood out to her the most). If your daughter needs help, feel free to offer suggestions.

Here's what I discovered in this session:

PERSONAL ACTION STEPS

Your daughter will record the personal changes she plans to make in her life as a result of what she has learned. Again, feel free to offer suggestions if she needs help.

NOTE: Have your daughter select one or two action points that she most wants to apply, and then have her write it (them) on the Personal Action Steps sheet on page 3 of her book.

Because my heart belongs to Him, I will:

keep moving

Over the next week try evaluating your spiritual and physical wardrobes.

A. How's your spiritual wardrobe looking? Does it need to be updated or improved? Or, is it in tip-top shape? Complete the following evaluation to find out the condition of your spiritual wardrobe. Ask the Lord to help you work on those areas where you need improvement, then faithfully work on those areas every day.

This section features additional projects. They are designed to help your daughter deepen her experience, and to encourage you to participate in her growth process. Feel free to use one or more of the assignments or projects presented, or use your creativity to create one or two of your own.

MY SPIRITUAL WARDROBE EVALUATION

	Looking Good	Needs Improvement	A Makeover Is in Order
Compassion			
Humility			
Kindness			
Gentleness			
Patience			
Forgiveness			
Love			
Joy			
Peace			
Faithfulness			
Self-Control			

B. Clean out your closet and take inventory of your clothes. Determine which items send the right messages and which ones may send the wrong messages. Separate the two, then box up and discard the ones that you determined may send the wrong messages, and neatly re-hang the ones that send the right messages. Be sure to mend or alter those items of clothing in need of repair.

Session 3

Learning to Communicate and Resolve Conflict

*Let the words of my mouth and
the meditation of my heart
be acceptable in Your sight,
O Lord, my rock and my Redeemer.*

Psalm 19:14

Reflection

To review the previous session and to follow up on projects and assignments, ask your daughter these four questions:

1. Thinking back over the previous session, what life-changing truth would you say stood out most to you?

2. How are you doing on your "Personal Action Steps" from the last session?

3. What progress have you made with your "Keep Moving" assignments and/or projects from the previous session? (Be sure to encourage her to complete those assignments or projects that she has not yet completed.)

4. Is there anything else from the previous session that you would like to talk about?

Focus

Good communication and conflict resolution skills can help you build relationships that you can enjoy for a lifetime.

OBJECTIVES:

You will help your daughter learn good communication skills and how to appropriately deal with conflict as you guide her to:

- Understand the importance of good communication for building healthy relationships.

- Examine the results of poor communication in relationships.

- Define conflict and its purpose.

- Evaluate how well she controls her tongue.

- Examine what the Bible has to say about the power of the tongue.

- Learn tips for better talks.

- Discover seven ground rules for dealing with conflict.

- Learn tips for better listening.

get ready

THE MISUNDERSTANDING, PART 1

This section features a fictional story and related discussion questions. It introduces your daughter to the topic and sparks an interest in the material to be covered in this session. Read the story aloud together, then discuss the questions.

Rebecca had been irritable all day. She was so relieved when the school day finally came to a close. The school bell was like music to her ears. As she bent over to tie her shoelaces, John rushed by her desk and accidentally knocked her backpack to the floor. Startled by the noise, she jumped up, but by the time she turned around John was gone and Haley was stepping over her backpack.

"Pick it up, Haley!" Rebecca shouted. Haley quickly looked around in embarrassment as Rebecca's shouting got the attention of the other kids in the room. Trying to save face, she yelled back, "I didn't knock it over!" That made Rebecca really angry, so she shouted at Haley again, and the girls began to argue, until finally Rebecca shouted, "Fine! I have nothing else to say to you!"

When Haley arrived at home, her mother could tell that she was upset. "What's wrong, Haley?" she asked with concern.

"Rebecca's mad at me."

"Why? What happened today between you two?"

"Rebecca accused me of doing something I didn't do, then we got into a big argument."

After Haley explained what happened, her mother said, "I'm really sorry to hear that. I know it doesn't feel good to be at odds with your best friend. And I know you think that you didn't do anything wrong."

"But I didn't!" said Haley interrupting. "She yelled at me first, and for no reason!"

"Yes, but you yelled at her too. My grandmother used to always say, 'It takes two to tango. If there's an argument, there are two people at fault.'"

Haley's mom paused, and then said, "You know, I've learned a lot about communication through my own mistakes. And I've found that there is a right way and a wrong way to communicate and to handle disagreements. The Bible says in Proverbs 15:1, "A gentle answer turns away wrath, but a harsh word stirs up anger." In light of this Scripture, how could you have responded differently when Rebecca yelled at you?"

"Well I probably shouldn't have yelled back at her," said Haley ashamedly. "I could have explained in a nice way that I didn't knock over her backpack. I guess I could have even picked it up for her."

My Heart Belongs to Him — My Identity

"And how do you think she might have reacted if you had responded that way?"

"She probably would have apologized to me for accusing me of knocking it over, and she probably wouldn't be mad at me." Then after a brief pause Haley said, "I guess I really blew it. Now what do I do?"

To be continued …

let's talk about it

1. What did you think of Rebecca's reaction when she saw her backpack on the floor and Haley stepping over it?

2. Would you have reacted like Haley did after being falsely accused? Why or why not?

3. Have you ever experienced an incident like Haley and Rebecca, where things got out of control as you tried to express yourself while handling a disagreement? What happened? What could you have done differently?

get real

THE IMPORTANCE OF GOOD COMMUNICATION

Communicating and interacting with others is something you do all the time, whether you are at home, at school, playing a sport, or shopping at the mall. Learning good communication skills will help you understand and relate to other people, and will help them to understand and get along with you. In addition, these skills will also help you to work out conflicts or differences you may have with others, in positive ways. Without good communication families can fall apart, friends can become enemies, people can become divided, and life's challenges can become unbearable.

Misunderstanding and conflict can occur between people because of poor communication. Sometimes it's because they were not clear in communicating what they wanted or how they were feeling. Sometimes it's because one person isn't really listening when the other person is talking. Often, people blurt out mean things when they are angry, or resort to lying or gossiping about others. And sometimes people stop speaking to each other all together. Rather than talking through their disagreement, they choose to give each other "the silent treatment."

let's talk about it

1. Why do you think people have a hard time communicating and expressing their feelings?

   Here are a few reasons people give:

   • I'm afraid I won't be accepted as I am.

   • I'm afraid I won't be understood.

   • I don't think people will really listen to me.

   • I don't trust others very much.

   • I don't feel my opinion will be valued.

   • I don't think others really care about what I have to say or about what's going on with me.

   • People don't really give me a chance to express myself.

2. What do you think can happen when two people who are having a disagreement don't take the time to listen and hear each other out?

3. Based on your own experience, how can "the silent treatment" make a conflict or disagreement worse?

4. How do you think good communication skills can improve your relationships?

Communicating With Parents and Siblings

Another area of communication that many teenagers struggle with is communicating with parents and with brothers and sisters. Have you ever hesitated in talking to your parents when you were experiencing a problem or facing a decision, and asked a friend for advice instead? What about when you disagreed with your parents' rules or a decision they made? Were you able to express your disagreement respectfully? Or did you blurt out things that you really didn't mean like "You never let me do anything!" or "You always say no!"

And let's face it; brothers and sisters don't always get along. They are often speaking to one another in harsh tones, teasing, name-calling, or hardly speaking to each other at all. But there is a better way! Knowing how to communicate the right way can help keep your relationships with your parents, siblings, and others alive and healthy—including your relationship with God.

let's talk about it

1. Why do you think teenagers often seek advice from their peers instead of talking to their parents? Do friends always give good advice? Why or why not?

Tip:
This is a great opportunity to help your daughter understand that because her friends are also in need of guidance and wise counsel, and are usually just as insecure, they cannot always give good advice. God gives children parents to help them process life. Parents have already traveled the road their children are on; therefore, they are more knowledgeable, more experienced, and better able to give wise counsel.

You can help your daughter understand that the more she communicates with you as her parents, the closer you become involved in each other's lives. Explain that when the lines of communication are kept open between you, she can feel safe with you and free to be herself. This makes it easier for her to open up with you about everything going on in her life, which helps you to do a better job of guiding and protecting her.

2. Do you think that it's important for teenagers and parents to talk and share often and openly? Why or why not?

Suggested answer: In order to give teens the counsel they need, it is important that parents know about their teenager's life, activities, and friends. The more they know, the wiser their counsel.

3. Have you ever said things to your parents or siblings that you didn't mean? How do you think that made them feel? How did it make you feel?

4. How can good communication skills improve your relationship with your parents? How can you improve the way you talk to and communicate with your brothers and sisters?

THE CHALLENGE OF DEALING WITH CONFLICT

How often have you heard or said these words: "I'm not speaking to you!" "I don't want to hear it!" "You're wrong. It's all your fault!" "You're such a loser!" "You never … !" "You always … !"

How often have you witnessed friends at school giving each other "the silent treatment"? Or best friends going their own separate ways after saying words like, "I'll never speak to you again!" How often have you seen two people yelling at each other because they can't agree about something? Or talk about each other behind each other's back, whispering and gossiping with others? And what about the times when someone uses words to put someone else down, tease others, or call someone names? Have you ever done any of those things when you were angry or dealing with a conflict or disagreement?

Conflict is a normal part of everyday life. What really matters is how you respond to it. When handled the right way, conflict can teach you how to relate to other people (including difficult people), how to appreciate their differences, how to be sensitive to their needs, and how to love, forgive, and trust. Relationships can become stronger as you work successfully through your differences. But if handled the wrong way (or if left unresolved), conflict can bring about hurt, pain, and bitterness, and it can strain and even destroy close friendships.

Tip:
This is a great time to explain to your daughter the reason why conflict arises in relationships. Because relationships are made up of two or more unique individuals with different backgrounds, values, personalities, and in many cases races, gender, or religions, there will be differences of opinion. Differing views about how to dress, what to eat, when to worship, what music to listen to, what movies to watch, and what extracurricular activities to be involved in can all cause conflict between people.

let's talk about it

1. Look at the following three examples of differences in friendships. In what ways can these differences cause conflict in each case?

   a. One person is outgoing, while the other is the quiet, shy type.

b. One person is from a wealthy family, while the other is from a poor family.

c. One has a strong faith in God, while the other does not.

2. How do you handle conflict in your relationships? Do you insist on having your own way? Or are you willing to give in, or compromise? Do you always avoid conflict at all costs?

3. Do you force your opinion on others, while criticizing theirs? Or do you hear the other person out? Is winning an argument your primary goal, or is making peace your main goal?

4. Try to recall a time when you handled conflict the right way. Share what happened, how you handled it, and what were the results? What about when you handled conflict the wrong way? Share what happened then, how you handled it improperly and what were the results? Do you see the difference? Explain.

HOW WELL CONTROLLED IS YOUR TONGUE?

One of the keys to having good communication skills is having a tongue that is well controlled. A tongue that is in control can speak words that are helpful to those who are listening, whereas a tongue that is out of control is one that blurts out words that are hurtful. This exercise will help you evaluate how well controlled your tongue is. Rate yourself on a scale of 1 to 10, 10 being best.

_____1. I build others up and encourage them, rather than tear down, belittle, or discourage them.

_____2. I say more positive things about people or situations rather than dwell on negative things.

_____3. I take time to think before I speak.

_____4. When someone confides in me, they can be assured I will keep that information safe.

_____5. I avoid participating in gossip.

_____6. I make a habit of telling the truth, even when telling the truth is difficult.

_____7. When I am angry, I am careful not to blurt out harsh remarks. Instead, I carefully choose my words, and then respond calmly.

_____8. I do not talk back to my parents or others in authority.

_____9. I avoid complaining, and tend to be thankful in any situation.

_____10. I ask God to help me keep my words pure every day.

- If your score was 80-100, you're doing a great job controlling your tongue!

- A score of 60-79 indicates your tongue is well controlled, but there is room for improvement.

- If your score was under 60, you are struggling in the area of controlling your tongue, and you need to make some immediate changes.

let's talk about it

1. What areas do you need to improve to better control your tongue?

2. Write out three action points for what you can do this week to better control your tongue.

let's pray about it

Talk with God and ask Him to help you learn how to communicate with others on a personal level—face to face—and how to handle conflict in ways that will help you grow and build strong personal relationships.

STOP HERE! If you prefer to do this session in two parts, you may find this to be a natural place to stop. However, if you want to complete this session in one sitting, please continue.

get direction

This section provides a clear picture of what the Bible has to say about this topic. The biblical truths and principles examined in this section will help your daughter apply God's Word to her life.

When you have good communication skills you will be better able to openly express your thoughts, feelings, and frustrations, and to properly work through conflicts. Knowing how to face difficult people and difficult situations will help you as you go through life. You will also be able to build solid relationships and friendships—where you can give and receive loyalty, trust, acceptance, and love, and where you can help one another grow.

In order to build those kinds of relationships, you must learn to communicate face to face. God doesn't want you to hide behind telephones, computers, or e-mail where no one can see or get to know the real you. Nor does He want you to rely on television, radio, or magazines to stay in touch with what's going on around you. With modern technology, it is so easy to avoid those calls or people we may feel are difficult, time consuming, or unimportant. However, it is very important that we learn how to deal with difficult people and difficult situations as we go through life.

My Heart Belongs to Him — My Identity

It is true that modern technology can be great, but it's important to learn how to use it to your advantage, without allowing it to stunt your growth, and without allowing it to take you away from spending quality time with God, your family, and friends. Communicating face to face is what will help you build and establish meaningful relationships that you can enjoy for a lifetime.

let's talk about it

1. In what ways do you think modern technology could stunt your growth?

2. How much time are you spending communicating with people using telephones, pagers, e-mail, instant messaging, and other remote technology?

3. Are you investing enough time building relationships by communicating face to face and by allowing people to get to know the real you? If not, what can you do differently?

THE POWER OF THE TONGUE

The Bible teaches that the tongue is very powerful. Proverbs 18:21a says, "Death and life are in the power of the tongue." Every time you open your mouth to speak, you have the power to hurt someone or to help someone. You can choose to say mean things or nice things. You can choose to laugh and tease someone or to encourage them. You can choose to give bad advice or to give good advice. And you can choose to argue your opinion or to patiently talk out disagreements. The choice is yours.

In James 3, verse 6, the tongue is compared to fire. Just as a small flame that is in control is not harmful, neither is a tongue that is in control. Think of a campfire. When it is in control it can be helpful and desirable. It can warm your body on cool nights, and it can warm your heart as you gather around its flame with family and friends. But if that small flame goes out of control, it can destroy acres and acres of land and homes, and can even kill wildlife and people.

It is the same with the tongue. When the tongue is in control it can warm hearts with kind, loving, and encouraging words. But when the tongue is out of control, it can be like a wildfire, spreading rapidly and causing damage wherever it goes.

Having control of your own tongue at all times is very important. We are told in 1 Peter 3:10 (TLB), "If you want a happy, good life, keep control of your tongue, and guard your lips from telling lies." However, controlling your tongue is something that is only possible with God's help. As James says in James 3:8 (TLB), "But no human being can tame the tongue. It is always ready to pour out its deadly poison."

Tip:
Your daughter might ask how could someone "cause death" by the words they speak. You can explain that hurtful words can cause death to a person's self-esteem, to their happiness, or a friendship.

let's talk about it

1. What does Jesus say about the importance of the words we speak in Matthew 12:36?

Suggested answer: Jesus warns us that God will hold us accountable for the things that we say.

2. Read Ephesians 4:29-31. Now make a list of careless words or unwholesome talk.

   Suggested answers: Lying, gossiping, complaining, cutting people down, profanity, making fun of others, talking negatively about someone when they are not around, being critical of others, saying mean things that can hurt someone's feelings, whispering, arguing, talking back to parents or others in authority, whining, and so on.

3. Which wound do you think might hurt more and take longer to heal: a physical wound (such as a scraped knee or a black eye) or an emotional wound (such as a broken heart as a result of hurtful words—gossiping, lying, name-calling, or teasing)? Why?

4. Can you think of a time when someone hurt you by something he or she said?

5. Now think of a time when you hurt someone else by something you said.

THINK BEFORE YOU SPEAK

1 Corinthians 2:16b says, "But we have the mind of Christ." Having the mind of Christ means that you keep yourself aware of what Jesus would think, say, or do at any moment if He were in your shoes. When your heart belongs to God, Jesus is the Lord of your life and His Holy Spirit lives in

Tip:
Just as your daughter can use an answering machine to screen her calls, she can use her mind to screen her words. God's Word gives us a great measuring stick to help us in the screening process. If our thoughts do not line up with God's Word—if they would not be pleasing to the Lord—then we know that those are not thoughts that we should acknowledge, recall, or speak. We can then choose to say something that is more in line with God's Word, something that would be helpful, not harmful, to the hearers and to ourselves.

you. Therefore, He is, in a sense, in your shoes. Take the time to think before you speak. Ask yourself, "What would Jesus want me to say or do in this situation?" You can prepare yourself in advance to answer that question by getting to know Jesus on a personal level (through prayer, Bible study, regular church attendance, participation in Sunday school, youth group, and through spending time with other Christians).

Whenever you are communicating with another person, let Psalm 19:14 be your guide: "Let the words of my mouth and the meditation of my heart be acceptable in Your sight, O Lord, my rock and my Redeemer." The best things to fill your heart with are God's love, peace, joy, compassion for others, and other positive qualities. Then the words you speak will also be acceptable. Luke 6:45c (TLB) tells us why: "Whatever is in the heart, overflows into speech."

get going

This is the life application section of the session. It includes practical guidelines and action points to help your daughter live out what she has learned.

TIPS FOR BETTER TALKS

- Consider what God's Word says about the tongue and how we should talk to one another and ask for God's help.
- Learn to honestly and lovingly express your thoughts, feelings, needs, and frustrations.
- Choose words, expressions, and voice tones that are kind and gentle. Don't use speech that could easily hurt someone or spark an argument.
- Refuse to allow bitterness or anger to control your speech.
- Make sure your body language is warm and personal, not threatening.
- Don't exaggerate or stretch the truth.
- Avoid being general; give specific examples.
- Choose an appropriate time to talk.

Try this for fun:

Take a few special moments to talk about some of the differences between the two of you. Contrast your differences by pointing out at least five things that you admire about each other, that make you different from each other—for example: personality traits, strengths, views, values, and so on. You might want to start by saying, "These are some of the things that I admire about you that make you uniquely you ... "

My Heart Belongs to Him — My Identity

Seven Ground Rules for Dealing with Conflict

1. **Understand and appreciate each other's differences.** Learn to value and appreciate each person as a unique individual with God-given gifts, talents and abilities; and respect others' opinions and views, even if you don't always agree with them.

2. **Learn to control angry feelings.** Ephesians 4:26 says, "Be angry, and yet do not sin; do not let the sun go down on your anger." It's okay to get angry. Anger is a God-given emotion. What's important is knowing how to handle those angry feelings properly. The first thing you should do is to admit that you are feeling angry. Realizing it's okay to feel the way you do, ask yourself why you are angry. Then talk to God about your anger, and ask Him to help you handle your feelings the right way. With His help and, if necessary, the help of a person you trust and respect, like Mom or Dad, do what you can to fix the problem.

3. **Make peace your goal.** God wants you to experience peace and unity in all of your relationships. Romans 12:18 says, "If possible, so far as it depends on you, be at peace with all men." When peace is your goal rather than winning, conflict can help to build up your relationship rather than tear it down. And remember that God wants us to settle our disagreements before the end of the day (Ephesians 4:26b) and before we offer our service to Him or prayers of thanksgiving (see Matthew 5:23-24). Avoiding conflict or hiding behind silence doesn't pay off. It only makes matters worse.

4. **Don't let pride get in the way.** Be fair, flexible, and willing to compromise. Proverbs 17:17a says, "A friend loves at all times." So remember, it is better to lose an argument than to lose a friendship—even if it means losing a little pride. Of course, you always need to stand firm in the truth, but share the truth in love.

Tip:
Encourage your daughter to carefully evaluate situations when conflict arises in her life, and to pray and ask God for help in making the right choices. You can explain to her these options for resolving conflict:
- **Accommodation:** You agree to change or give in.
- **Acceptance:** You accept the fact that the other person won't change.
- **Compromise:** You both agree to change by finding a middle ground.
- **Agree to disagree:** Neither of you will change your views on the subject of the disagreement, but both of you agree to move forward together.

Here are some helpful ways that you can share with your daughter for choosing her words carefully before she speaks:

- **Examine your thoughts.** Are they in obedience to Jesus Christ (2 Corinthians 10:5)? If not, reject those thoughts. Refuse to entertain them.

- **Check your heart.** What are your motives for what you have to say? Is your heart pure before God? In Matthew 12:34b the Bible says, "For the mouth speaks out of that which fills the heart."

- **Consider others as more important than yourself** (Philippians 2:3-4). Try harder to understand than to be understood.

- **Ask yourself, "What would Jesus say?"** Then respond accordingly. Philippians 2:5 says that our attitude should be the kind that was shown by Jesus Christ.

5. **Be a good listener.** When people take the time to listen to each other, they better understand one another. Listening also gives you time to calm down and evaluate your own thoughts and feelings. James 1:19b says, "But everyone must be quick to hear, slow to speak and slow to anger." In other words, we should listen more and talk less.

6. **Choose your words carefully.** One of the most important things to remember when you are settling a disagreement is to choose your words carefully. Avoid using words like "never" and "always." They are rarely true. Attack the problem—not the person.

7. **Be quick to forgive.** Ephesians 4:32 says, "Be kind to one another, tender-hearted, forgiving each other, just as God in Christ also has forgiven you." God commands us to forgive each other. When you forgive others you can experience more fully God's forgiveness in your own life. But not only does God want you to forgive ... He also wants you to leave it in the past. Isaiah 43:18 (NIV) says, "Forget the former things; do not dwell on the past." Once you have forgiven someone, you should not dwell on it. And if you are wrong, admit it, apologize, and ask for forgiveness from the other person and from God.

MORE TIPS FOR BETTER LISTENING: [1]

- Listen with an attitude that the other person's comments deserve your focused attention (which means that you shouldn't be playing a video game, listening to music, or watching TV while the other person is talking).

- Listen with the willingness to understand what the other person is saying, feeling, and needing.

- If necessary, ask questions for better understanding, and be sensitive to those needs that the other person is expressing.

- Listen with the understanding that the other person is not your enemy.

- Listen with the willingness to hear what God may be saying through the other person.

let's talk about it

Look at the following real-life situations. Using the information that you learned in this session, tell what you think would be the right way and the wrong way to respond in each case:

1. You and a friend are out shopping for matching outfits. You each find an outfit that you like, only she doesn't like the one you chose, and you don't care for the one she chose.

2. You and a friend try out for the cheerleading squad together. The next day, you and your friend run to the gym to look for your names on the posting of those who made it. Her name is there and yours isn't. You don't think it's fair—in fact, you thought you were a bit better at cheering than she was.

3. You and your sister want to watch different programs on television, and you begin arguing over who gets to hold the remote control.

4. Your sister wants to wear your favorite sweater, but you were planning to wear that sweater later on this evening. You tell her "no" in a nice way and you give her your reasons. But she yells at you saying things like, "You are so stingy! You never let me wear anything of yours!"

5. Your teacher yells at you to stop talking and threatens to send you to the office the next time you disrupt the class. Only, you were not the one who was talking—the two girls sitting next to you were. Everyone laughs and teases you.

THE MISUNDERSTANDING, PART 2 ...

Later that evening, Haley's mother drove her to Rebecca's house so that the two girls could resolve their conflict. When they arrived, Haley walked up to Rebecca's bedroom and sat next to her on the bed, and the girls began to talk.

"I'm sorry I yelled at you today, Rebecca," said Haley. " ... And even though I didn't knock over your backpack," she continued, "I could have picked it up for you."

"I'm sorry I yelled at you too, Haley," said Rebecca. "I was just really tired, and I had a horrible day. I took it out on you ... I was wrong."

"When you turned around and yelled at me," continued Haley, "I felt embarrassed in front of the other kids. And I knew I was being accused of something I didn't do. But I still should not have yelled at you."

"I'm sorry that what I did embarrassed you," said Rebecca. "Will you forgive me?" Haley smiled, then said, "Of course I will. Will you forgive me?"

Rebecca said yes, and then the girls hugged. "Oh, by the way," said

My Heart Belongs to Him — My Identity

Rebecca, "John told me that he accidentally knocked my backpack off the desk. He said he was sorry that he didn't pick it up, but he was in a rush to get to the bathroom. He said he really had to go!" The girls burst into laughter.

let's pray about it

Talk with God and ask Him to help you put into practice the good communication and conflict resolution skills you learned in this session, so that you can use your tongue to honor Him and to help others, even in the midst of conflict.

POINT OF DISCOVERY

Here your daughter will record the key principles that she has learned in this session (those truths that stood out to her the most). If your daughter needs help, feel free to offer suggestions.

Here's what I discovered in this session:

PERSONAL ACTION STEPS

Your daughter will record the personal changes she plans to make in her life as a result of what she has learned. Again, feel free to offer suggestions if she needs help.

NOTE: Have your daughter select one or two action points that she most wants to apply, and then have her write it (them) on the Personal Action Steps sheet on page 3 of her book.

Because my heart belongs to Him, I will:

keep moving

Here are some great activities for you to try:

A.   Evaluate a conflict you and your mom had recently. Discuss together how that conflict could have been resolved in a more peaceful way. Then role-play the conflict again using some of the conflict resolution skills that you learned in this session.

B.   Set aside a time when you can connect with your mom each day to talk and share with each other about the day. Share the highs and lows, prayer requests, praise reports, and whatever else may be on your hearts.

C.   Make a list of examples of unwholesome talk and post it near the telephone and on the refrigerator to help you remember to guard your tongue.

This section features additional projects. They are designed to help your daughter deepen her experience, and to encourage you to participate in her growth process. Feel free to use one or more of the assignments or projects presented, or use your creativity to create one or two of your own.

As You Deal With Conflicts in Friendships, Remember True Friends:

- Do not keep score.

- Are willing to apologize.

- Are willing to see the other person's point of view.

- Speak the truth in love, so as not to hurt but to help.

- Believe in each other.

- Want the best for each other.

- Do not hold grudges against each other, but forgive one another ... even for the little things.

- Hang in there with each other.

- Don't gossip about each other.

- Don't fight in public.

Session 4 *Choosing Friends Wisely*

*Don't be teamed with people
who do not love the Lord,
for what do the people of God
have in common with the people of sin?
How can light live with darkness?*

2 Corinthians 6:14 (TLB)

Reflection

To review the previous session and to follow up on projects and assignments, ask your daughter the following four questions:

1. Thinking back over the previous session, what life-changing truth would you say stood out most to you?

2. How are you doing on your "Personal Action Steps" from the last session?

3. What progress have you made with your "Keep Moving" assignments and/or projects from the previous session? (Be sure to encourage her to complete those assignments or projects that she has not yet completed.)

4. Is there anything else from the previous session that you would like to talk about?

Focus

Choosing friends is among the most important choices you will ever make as you live and grow, because friends often become like each other, influencing one another, either in positive or negative ways. Your friendships will affect the rest of your life.

OBJECTIVES:

You will help your daughter understand the importance of choosing her friends wisely as you guide her to:

- Understand the role that friendships play in our lives.

- Learn the different levels of friendship.

- Discover the makings of a true friend.

- Evaluate her closest friends in light of the makings of a true friend.

- Recognize character qualities to look for and to guard against when choosing friends.

- Learn ways to share Christ with non-Christian friends.

get ready

This section features a fictional story and related discussion questions. It introduces your daughter to the topic and sparks an interest in the material to be covered in this session. Read the story aloud together, then discuss the questions.

BIRDS OF A FEATHER

"Hey, Kaitlyn," shouted Karen as she and a group of girls passed her in the hall on the way to their next class, "What did you get on the test?"

"I got an 'A+', 100%!" Kaitlyn answered with pride.

"Too bad you had to cheat to get a good grade, Kaitlyn," teased one of the girls walking with Karen. Her words pierced Kaitlyn's heart like an arrow and made her angry. "I didn't cheat!" Kaitlyn quickly yelled back.

"Oh, sure you didn't," said one of the other girls, "Your two friends got caught! They're in the principal's office, right now. I wonder how you got away with it?"

"Yeah! How'd you pull it off, Kaitlyn?" said Karen accusingly.

"I didn't cheat!" Kaitlyn insisted, then stormed away to her next class.

After school, Kaitlyn saw Karen and her friends again. As they passed her on the way to their school bus, they laughed and pointed at her. She was so hurt that she no longer felt good about the perfect score that she received on her test. She began to feel as if all those late nights of studying with her sister, Haley, were a waste of time.

As soon as Kaitlyn walked through the front door, her mother yelled out, "Hi, Katie! How'd you do on your big test?"

"I don't want to talk about it!" she yelled back, bursting into tears. Then she ran to her room and slammed the door behind her.

Her mother stopped what she was doing and immediately went to talk to Kaitlyn.

"What happened?" she asked.

"It's just not fair!" Kaitlyn replied angrily. "I studied so hard for that test, and I got an 'A+'. Now just because Sharon and Alexis cheated, some of the kids are accusing me of cheating too! I earned that grade fair and square!"

"I'm really surprised at Alexis. That's not like her," said Mother disappointedly. "However, this is the second time this month you girls have gotten into trouble in connection with Sharon. It's obvious that she has some issues that she's struggling with. Her poor choices are causing problems in her own life, as well as creating a negative effect on people who hang out with her."

"I'm going to give Sharon's and Alexis' mothers a call so that we can discuss this entire situation. Meanwhile, until Sharon improves her behavior, I really don't think it's a good idea to spend so much time with her. As I've told you before, 'Birds of a feather, flock together.' Whatever reputation your friends have will be passed on to you, simply because you associate yourself with them. If you hang around with people who make a habit of doing bad things, others will think you do those bad things too."

"But it's not true!" Kaitlyn yelled tearfully.

"I know, honey," said Mother compassionately, "but again, people make judgments about you simply by the company you keep. It's called being guilty by association."

let's talk about it

1. How were Alexis' and Kaitlyn's reputations affected as a result of choosing Sharon as a friend?

2. What do you think Kaitlyn learned from this friendship experience? If you were Kaitlyn, how would you feel in this situation?

3. Have you ever been judged unfairly because of a friend's reputation? How did you handle it and what did you learn from the experience?

get real

Your friendships will affect the rest of your life. Friends help shape who you are and who you will become. Because of the close connection between people in a friendship, friends often become like each other—influencing one another in positive or negative ways. Friends can help you grow and become a better person, or they can bring you down, and even ruin your reputation. Friends can help you draw closer to Christ, or they can pull you toward sin. Friends can encourage you to do the right thing, or they can influence you to do wrong. That is why it is so important for you to choose your friends wisely and to know the difference between a real friend and one who is really not a friend at all.

THE IMPORTANCE OF FRIENDSHIP

Everyone wants and needs someone who they can call a friend. Without friends, life would be lonely and miserable. Think about it. What would life be like if you had no one with whom you could share things in common, no one with whom you could feel comfortable and be yourself, no one to help you celebrate the good times, and no one to lean on in the bad times? What would life be like if you had no one to hang out with and no one with whom you could spend time doing things that are fun and enjoyable? Scary thought isn't it?

let's talk about it

1. What are some of the benefits of having a friend who influences you in positive ways?

Tip:

You might want to share with your daughter that friends are not our only source of happiness, nor can they meet all of our needs. We can only find true happiness by having a right relationship with God. He is the Source of our self-worth, security, happiness, strength, peace, and joy. Matthew 5:3 says, "How happy are those who know their need for God, for the kingdom of Heaven is theirs!" (Phillips Translation). However, there are times when God will choose to use a friend to meet specific needs in our lives, but we are not to depend on them to meet all of our needs. When we understand that Christ is the Source for meeting all of our needs, we can lower our expectations of our friendships and we are freed up to give grace when mistakes are made.

2. What are the possible consequences of having a friend who influences you in negative ways?

THE MAKINGS OF A TRUE FRIEND

A true friend is like an ally—someone who will stand with you and support you no matter what. She is someone who accepts you for who you are—someone who appreciates your strengths and understands your weaknesses. A true friend is someone you can depend on in good times and bad—someone who treats you with love, compassion, kindness, and respect. You can expect loyalty from a true friend. When you share your secrets with her you can rest assured that she would not betray your confidences, and she has your best interests in mind when giving you advice. A true friend has a good reputation and will challenge you to make wise choices and to do the right thing. She will bring out the best in you, and will bear with you when you are not at your best.

A true friend will have fun with you, laugh with you, and cry with you when you are hurting. She is careful not to tease you in a mean way, laugh at you, put you down, lie, or gossip about you. In the midst of conflict, she would put your needs above her own and would be willing to compromise to make peace. A true friend genuinely apologizes to you when she hurts you or when she makes a mistake. And if you're wrong, she will lovingly correct you. A true friend is all of those things, and so much more. A true friend— especially one who loves the Lord—is a special treasure that everyone needs in life to grow and flourish.

let's talk about it

1. Evaluate your closest friends. Take a sheet of paper and list each by name. Then evaluate each friend using the following questions:

  a. Does she fit the description of a true friend given above?

  b. What areas do you feel she needs to improve as a friend?

  c. Would she be willing to improve?

  d. In what ways does she build you up?

  e. In what ways does she pull you down?

  f. Does she encourage you to make wise choices or wrong choices?

2. Based on your answers, do you think you have chosen your friends wisely? Explain

3. What about you? When others choose you for a friend are they making a wise choice?

4. How do you measure up to the description of a true friend? In what areas can you improve as a friend?

let's pray about it

Talk to God about your choices of friends. Ask Him to reveal to you those friends who are true friends and those who are not, and to help you to choose your friends wisely. Ask Him to help you to be a true friend to others as well—the type of friend that they can say they have chosen wisely.

STOP HERE! If you prefer to do this session in two parts, you may find this to be a natural place to stop. However, if you want to complete this session in one sitting, please continue.

My Heart Belongs to Him — My Identity

get direction

God created in us a longing for friends. As you learned earlier in this session, everyone wants and needs a friend. God brings special people into your life to help you grow and to influence and challenge you to make wise choices. Proverbs 27:17 (NIV) says, "As iron sharpens iron, so one man sharpens another." Because He loves you, He wants you to have someone with whom you can laugh, have fun, and enjoy life—someone who shares your values and love for Him. He wants you to have someone you can count on to be there for you in good times and bad. Ecclesiastes 4:9-12 (NIV) puts it this way: "Two are better than one, because they have a good return for their work. If one falls down his friend can help him up. But pity the man who falls and has no one to help him up!"

God knows how important friendship is. That's why He gave us some definite guidelines for choosing friends wisely. In 1 Corinthians 15:33 He warns us about hanging out with the wrong kind of people. The verse says, "Do not be deceived: 'Bad company corrupts good morals,'" telling you that when you have close friends who are foolish, worldly, or rebellious, you are asking for trouble. Therefore, you should not hang out with someone who has a bad reputation, makes poor choices (like drinking, smoking, using drugs, being disrespectful to adults, skipping classes, or using profanity), or who encourages you to do things that you know are wrong. That person is not a true friend and their influence can get you into a lot of trouble.

This section provides a clear picture of what the Bible has to say about this topic. The biblical truths and principles examined in this section will help your daughter apply God's Word to her life.

let's talk about it

1. Read 2 Corinthians 6:14. Why do you think God warns us to be careful about the influence of people?

   Suggested answer: Because if they do not share your love for the Lord, they will not share the same values and morals. Their choices will not be made with God's guidance and will therefore most likely be poor choices, which could influence you in negative ways and get you into trouble, including the possibility of ruining your reputation.

2. Read 2 Timothy 3:2-4. From this Scripture, make a list of negative qualities the Bible warns us to guard against when choosing friends.

Suggested answer: Those negative qualities are: lovers of self, lovers of money, boastful, arrogant, revilers (abusive), disobedient to parents, ungrateful, unholy, unloving, irreconcilable (argumentative, not willing to give in), malicious gossips, without self-control, haters of good, treacherous, reckless, conceited, lovers of pleasure rather than lovers of God.

(Other Scriptures that list negative qualities to guard against: Proverbs 10:4, 11:13, 11:17, 12:17, 15:32, 20:3, 22:24,25; 25:19, 25:28, 27:4, 29:22.)

3. Think about your own friends. Do your friends have any of those negative qualities? If so, how might those friendships be affecting your life?

SPECIAL FRIENDSHIPS

2 Corinthians 6:14 emphasizes that we are not to be "yoked together" with unbelievers. This means we are not to be closely linked with, fastened to, connected with, or attached to someone who does not know Jesus, which means that you should not have unbelievers as your closest friends.

However, as a Christian, you do have a responsibility to share Jesus with unbelievers. God wants you to have a heart for the lost (those who do not know Him). It is therefore acceptable for you to have an unbeliever as a casual friend, so that you can share your faith and be a living example of God's love.

If you know someone who is not a Christian, one of the most effective ways you can share Christ with them is by the way you live your life. Let Jesus shine through you in the choices you make, in the way you treat others, in your attitude, and in all that you do. You can also share God's love by being there to help when that person is in need or struggling with a problem. And it would be a great idea to include him or her in get-togethers with other Christians at lunches, ball games, and other events. Also, extend an invitation to attend youth group and church. If you allow the light of Jesus to shine through your words and actions, your friends will most likely want to know Him too. For helpful tips on how to introduce your friend to Christ, see the "Keep Moving" section at the end of this session.

If your friend is not interested in becoming a Christian, don't feel badly. Sometimes God chooses to use one person to plant a seed and sends someone else along to water it. In other words, He might use you to get that person to start thinking about Christianity. And He might use someone else to help that person make a decision to follow Christ. No matter what part you play, it is an honor to be used by God in the lives of other people. Continue to pray for that person and continue to be a godly example.

let's talk about it

1. Can people see Jesus in you? How can you tell?

2. Has your relationship with Jesus influenced your friends? If yes, in what ways?

3. What are some ways that you can do a better job of sharing God's love and of setting a godly example for your friends?

REACHING OUT TO THE UNPOPULAR

There also are many people who need friends. Perhaps there's someone you know who doesn't seem to quite fit in. You know—the one who stands alone at school, eats alone, and never gets picked to participate in games or to play on a sports team. Or the one who never gets invited to parties, sleepovers or other activities—the person everyone calls gross, weird, loner, or outcast. If you know someone who fits that description, then you know someone who is probably hurting, afraid, and feeling very alone. He or she needs the blessing of friendship.

In Matthew 25:40 (NIV) Jesus tells us, " … I tell you the truth, whatever you did for one of the least of these brothers of mine, you did for me." God shows His favor on those who reach out to others with His love.

 let's talk about it

1. Is there someone you know who might need a friend? Would you consider giving him or her the gift of friendship?

2. What can you do this week to begin forming a friendship with this person?

WHO'S INFLUENCING WHOM?

The important thing to remember is that we become like those we spend time with. If you spend a lot of time with people who do not share your commitment to Christ, you will either influence them—pulling them toward a relationship with Christ—or they will influence you—pulling you toward sin and unwise choices. For an example of how the influence of an unbelieving friend can affect you, take a look into Samson's life (Judges 13-16).

My Heart Belongs to Him — My Identity

Samson's greatest weakness was that he allowed others to influence him. He gave in to the pressures of his unbelieving friends (read Judges 16:4-21). Even though he had a lot going for him, he suffered great loss because of those negative influences. He lost his strength, his anointing, his eyesight, his freedom, his honor, and eventually ... his life.

If you find that your non-Christian friends are influencing you in negative ways, instead of you influencing them in positive ways, it would be in your best interest to back away from those friendships right away. With Mom's help, write out a plan to lovingly back away from those friends who may be causing you to sin or who may be causing you to compromise your commitment to Christ. Then pray and ask God to give you the strength to follow through, and do so right away. Remember to keep that friend on your prayer list and to be faithful to pray for him or her. Because God loves them, He will be sure to send someone else to help that person move closer to Him.

let's talk about it

1. Why is it important to form casual friendships with non-Christians?

   Suggested answer: It is important to form relationships with those who may not know Christ for the purpose of sharing your faith and setting a godly example.

2. What are some ways that you can influence those friends?

   Suggested answer: You can influence those friends by being a godly example, by challenging them to make right choices, by suggesting positive alternatives to negative activities, and by sharing with them about your faith in Jesus.

3. What are some ways that non-Christian friends can influence you?

   Suggested answer: If you spend a lot of time with non-Christian friends, you can become numb to negative behaviors and possibly begin to imitate them yourself. If you're not strong enough, they can influence you to make poor choices as they apply negative peer pressure.

Tip:
Walking away from people we consider "friends," even though they may not be good for us, can be very difficult, especially for teenage girls. Give your daughter as much support and encouragement as she needs through this process, and help her find the strength to follow through. Pray with and for her often during this time, and follow-up with her progress. Encourage her to choose wisely as she meets people and develops new friends. Remind her to use the biblical guidelines for choosing friends that she learned in this session.

4. Why is it important for you to back away from those friends who are influencing you in negative ways?

    Suggested answer: To guard your moral purity and to keep you from compromising your standards and your relationship with Christ.

5. What does Proverbs 12:26 tell us about being cautious in our friendships?

    Suggested answer: This verse tells us that the righteous (people of God) can offer guidance to others, but that the wicked can lead people astray (in the wrong direction). We should therefore be careful, as God's people, to influence others in positive ways. We do not want to be influenced or led by those who are making wrong choices and traveling in the wrong direction.

get going

This is the life application section of the session. It includes practical guidelines and action points to help your daughter live out what she has learned.

You know how picky we girls can be when we go shopping for clothes. We are usually very careful about which outfits we choose for ourselves. As you look at the different colors and styles, have you ever asked yourself, "Is this the best outfit for me? What will wearing this outfit say about me? What will others think?" As you know, you are judged by your outer appearance every day. But even more than what you wear, people will make judgments about you according to who you spend your time with. For example, if you hang around with a person who has a reputation for stealing, people will automatically believe that you steal too (even if you don't) and will have a hard time trusting you. You want to therefore choose friends who have a reputation that you and others can admire.

Just as you ask yourself certain questions while you shop for your clothing, here are some important questions you can ask yourself as you choose your friends. Questions like:

- Does she have a growing relationship with the Lord?
- Is this the best person for me to spend time with? What kind of reputation does she have?
- Will she help me grow and become a better person? Will I be able to help her do the same?
- What are my reasons for choosing her for a friend?
- Will my parents approve of our friendship? Why? Why not?

These questions can help you choose your friends wisely. Depending upon your answers, you can determine whether or not you should develop a close friendship with a person, or whether you should form a casual friendship in order to share Christ. You may determine that it would be best for you to avoid someone's company altogether but be faithful to pray for that person, knowing that God will send someone other than you into his or her life to draw them closer to Him.

A Description of Qualities to Look For When Choosing Friends

Because your heart belongs to God, these are the qualities you should look for in a young woman with whom you can share a close friendship:

1. She is excited about her relationship with Christ and He is number 1 in her life. You don't even have to ask her if she is a Christian. You can tell by watching her life.

   > "… love the Lord your God with all your heart, and with all your soul, and with all your mind, and with all your strength."
   >
   > Mark 12:30

Tip:
These qualities of a true friend are also good traits for parents to imitate.

2. She shows unconditional love towards others, and is loyal even when they are unlovable.

   > A friend loves at all times.
   >
   > Proverbs 17:17a

3. She is forgiving when others have offended her.

   Be kind and compassionate to one another, forgiving each other, just as in Christ God forgave you.

   Ephesians 4:32 (NIV)

4. She admits her faults and apologizes when she makes mistakes.

   Therefore, confess your sins to one another, and pray for one another so that you may be healed.

   James 5:16a

5. She is not selfish or self-centered. She joyfully gives of herself and is concerned about the needs of others.

   Do nothing out of selfish ambition or vain conceit, but in humility consider others better than yourselves. Each of you should look not only to your own interests, but also to the interests of others.

   Philippians 2:3-4 (NIV)

6. She can be trusted with secrets.

   A gossip betrays a confidence, but a trustworthy man keeps a secret.

   Proverbs 11:13 (NIV)

7. She keeps her promises.

   God delights in those who keep their promises, and abhors those who don't.

   Proverbs 12:22 TLB

8. She is able to resist or run away from temptation.

   Submit therefore yourselves, then, to God. Resist the devil, and he will flee from you.

   James 4:7

   Now flee from youthful lusts and pursue righteousness, faith, love and peace, with those who call on the Lord from a pure heart.

   2 Timothy 2:22

9. She does not have close friends who drink alcohol, smoke, use drugs, steal, or who have bad reputations.

> *Abstain from all appearance of evil.*
>
> 1 Thessalonians 5:22 (KJV)

10. She is not controlled by anger or by her temper.

> *Like a city whose walls are broken down is a man who lacks self-control.*
>
> Proverbs 25:28 (NIV)

These are not unrealistic standards for a friend who is following Jesus Christ and whose heart belongs to Him. However, no one has perfected all of these qualities. Everyone is at a different level of maturity. But a friend who is working toward being more like Jesus is a friend worth having. And always remember, you have to work at becoming the right kind of friend in order to have the right kind of friends. You learned in the story "Birds of a Feather" that people with similar interests, values, and beliefs are usually drawn to each other. If you are demonstrating godly qualities in your life, people with similar qualities will be drawn to you.

 let's talk about it

1. Take a few moments to evaluate yourself using the qualities above.

2. Which qualities are most evident in your life?

3. Choose two of the above qualities and share specific times when you demonstrated those qualities in your friendships.

4. Which qualities do you need to work at the most?

let's pray about it

Ask God to help you develop and live out the positive, godly qualities of a true friend as you relate to others. Pray also that God would bring other young people into your life who have growing relationships with the Lord. And ask Him to give you wisdom in your friendships with non-Christian friends.

Here's what I discovered in this session:

POINT OF DISCOVERY

Here your daughter will record the key principles that she has learned in this session (those truths that stood out to her the most). If your daughter needs help, feel free to offer suggestions.

Because my heart belongs to Him, I will:

PERSONAL ACTION STEPS

Your daughter will record the personal changes she plans to make in her life as a result of what she has learned. Again, feel free to offer suggestions if she needs help.

NOTE: Have your daughter select one or two action points that she most wants to apply, and then have her write it (them) on the Personal Action Steps sheet on page 3 of her book.

keep moving

This section features additional projects designed to help your daughter deepen her experience as she works through this study, and to encourage you to participate in her growth process. Feel free to use one or more of the assignments or projects presented, or use your creativity to create one or two of your own.

A. Look again at your evaluation of your closest friends that you completed earlier in the session. Discuss your answers with Mom. Then decide together if you need to make any adjustments in your friendships.

B. Pray and ask God to strengthen your true friendships and to give you the desire and the strength to break away from those friendships that are not good for you.

C. To break away from a negative friendship, ask Mom to help you write out a plan to lovingly back away. Then prayerfully follow through with your plan, and remember to continue to pray for that friend.

D. To share Christ with a non-Christian friend, see the helpful tips below, and refer to the appendix entitled "You Can Know God Personally." Then, write out a plan to introduce your friend to Jesus. Go over your plan with Mom, and role-play it together a few times. Remember to pray before approaching your friend.

HELPFUL TIPS FOR INTRODUCING A FRIEND TO JESUS CHRIST:

- Explain why you asked Him into your life (read Romans 3:23).
- Tell how knowing Him has made a difference in your life. Give examples of how Jesus has helped you and given you good advice through His Word, Sunday school, godly mentors, etc.
- Share the benefits of experiencing God's forgiveness (read 1 John 1:9).
- Be sure to tell how you spend time with the Lord, talking with Him about everything in prayer (read Philippians 4:6-7).
- Explain how He helps you to overcome fears and problems you may have (read 1 Corinthians 15:57).
- Say that because you love Him and are loyal to Him, you choose to live a life that is pleasing to Him (read 2 Timothy 2:19-22).

If your friend is ready (expresses a desire to know Jesus), introduce him or her to Jesus, using the steps in the appendix entitled "You Can Know God Personally." (If you do not feel comfortable doing this on your own, you can either invite your friend over to your house so Mom or Dad can help you introduce your friend to Jesus, or you can ask your youth leader to help you.)

After your friend receives Christ as Lord and Savior, you can help your friend grow closer to the Lord by inviting him or her to become a part of your church or youth group. (If your friend is a guy, connect him with a strong Christian young man with whom he can study God's Word and pray. A really important rule to follow is to have guys disciple guys and girls disciple girls. However, always remember to pray for him.)

If your friend is a girl, you could be a spiritual big sister to her. You can pray together and study God's Word together. This will help the two of you grow closer to the Lord and to each other. And remember to pray for your friend often because others will attempt to hold her back as she seeks to follow Christ and begins to make changes in her life.

Session 5

Surviving the Squeeze of Peer Pressure

*Be strong in the Lord,
and in the power of his might.*
Ephesians 6:10b (KJV)

Reflection

To review the previous session and to follow up on projects and assignments, ask your daughter the following four questions:

1. Thinking back over the previous session, what life-changing truth would you say stood out most to you?

2. How are you doing on your "Personal Action Steps" from the last session?

3. What progress have you made with your "Keep Moving" assignments and/or projects from the previous session? (Be sure to encourage her to complete those assignments or projects that she has not yet completed.)

4. Is there anything else from the previous session that you would like to talk about?

Focus

Because friendships are so important throughout the teenage years and because you have a natural need to be loved and accepted, peer pressure—whether positive or negative—can be a powerful influence in your life.

OBJECTIVES:

You will help your daughter learn practical ways to deal with negative peer pressure and to challenge others with positive peer pressure as you guide her to:

- Understand the difference between positive peer pressure and negative peer pressure, and the possible consequences of each.

- Evaluate her peers and determine which kind of peer pressure she is receiving more of.

- With God's help, face and overcome the fear of standing up for what is right, even when she may have to stand alone.

- Be strong in the Lord, and learn how to use the spiritual armor to resist the enemy.

- Learn four practical steps to overcome negative peer pressure in her daily life.

This section features a fictional story and related discussion questions. It introduces your daughter to the topic and sparks an interest in the material to be covered in this session. Read the story aloud together, then discuss the questions.

THE TESTIMONY

The room was completely quiet as Dillon gave his testimony before the youth group. With tears in his eyes, Dillon talked about what happened to him when he gave in to pressure from two of his buddies to try cigarettes, which eventually led to marijuana. He began to sob as he shared with the group how drugs took over his life, affecting his grades, his performance on the basketball team, and his relationship with his parents.

As Dillon shared, Kaitlyn drifted into deep thought. She thought about how she had given in to pressure from a couple of girls at school to wear make-up, even though her parents had forbidden her to do so until ninth grade. And even then, she would only be allowed to wear light make-up. When she told Pamela and Nikki what her parents said, they laughed. "Your parents are so old-fashioned!" Pamela had said. After constant pressure from the two girls, Kaitlyn began to wear make-up at school. Three months later, those same girls had succeeded in getting her to try cigarettes.

Tears filled Kaitlyn's eyes as she recalled the feelings of guilt she experienced every day when she came home from school and faced her parents, knowing she had disobeyed them. She recalled how her quiet time with the Lord had gone from every day to maybe once a week, and even then she didn't feel close to the Lord anymore. Then she began to wonder how far she would allow the girls to take her. First make-up, now cigarettes … what next? She thought to herself. Would I end up on drugs with my life in ruins like Dillon did?

Later on that evening, Hailey could tell something was bothering her younger sister. "What's up, Katie?" she asked. "You've been acting weird ever since Dillon gave his testimony. Was it something he said?"

"Well, sort of, but I really don't want to talk about it right now."

"Katie, is something going on that I don't know about?"

Kaitlyn hung her head and shrugged her shoulders. She was really ashamed and too embarrassed to talk about it. "I said, I don't want to talk about it right now," she said sadly. "Maybe some other time."

"Okay, well whatever it is, Katie, just know that I'm here for you, and Mom and Dad are too. Maybe you'll feel better if you talk to them." Kaitlyn's eyes widened as she shook her head no. "Well, maybe you feel that way right now, but trust me, whatever it is they'll understand," Hailey said. "They always do when I do the wrong things. You might get in trouble at first, but they will help you in the end. They always help me."

Kaitlyn let out a loud sigh, then rested her head in her hands. "And by the way," continued Hailey, "you know that you can always talk to God."

let's talk about it

1. Do you think it would have been easier for Kaitlyn to say no to cigarettes if she had said no to the pressure to wear make-up?

2. Why do you think she gave in to Pamela and Nikki when they pressured her to do things she knew were wrong? Where might her friendship with Pamela and Nikki eventually lead her?

3. What changes do you think Kaitlyn might have made in her life after the night of Dillon's testimony? How can she make a difference in her friends' lives?

get real

Tip:

For fun, see how many advertisements, TV programs, movies, songs, and music videos you can think of that pressure teenagers to do things that are not right. (For example: programs with teens talking to adults disrespectfully, using profanity, drinking, or getting involved in sexual relationships; programs or commercials with sensual themes or messages like "just do it," "no rules."

For deeper understanding, ask your daughter how many of her peers are doing things that they know are wrong (and don't really want to do) just so they can fit in? Does she think that what they are doing is worth the results they are getting? Do they appear to be rising to the top or sinking to the bottom, trading in their reputations and self-respect to gain popularity or the approval of the "in crowd"?

No one wants to be teased, laughed at, or shut out of a group. How many kids do you know who are willing to do what everyone else is doing, just to fit in? It's hard to be different—to go against the crowd. The pressure of wanting to be liked, or considered cool, causes many students to allow their friends to make decisions for them—even when those decisions may not be right. For many young people during the teenage years, fitting in can sometimes be more important than doing what is right.

Teenagers today are under so much pressure not only from peers, but also from television, music, magazines, billboards, and other media. Voices are calling out all around you with messages that say, "No Rules!" "No limits!" "Just do it!" Life can be so confusing.

TWO KINDS OF PEER PRESSURE

When you hear about peer pressure, it's usually the negative kind—the kind that encourages you to do things that you know are wrong, such as drink alcohol, cheat, steal, do drugs, lie, have pre-marital sex, or take on unattractive attitudes so that you can be considered cool. It's the kind of peer pressure that can cause you to become someone you're not, just to please others. This kind of peer pressure encourages you to take the easy way out and go with the flow—to do what "everyone else is doing" just to fit in.

Believe it or not, there is another kind of peer pressure. It's the positive kind—the kind of pressure from friends that encourages you to go against the flow, daring you to be different and to take a stand for doing what is right. Whereas negative peer pressure can pull you away from Christ and push you toward sin, positive peer pressure does just the opposite. It pushes you toward Christ and helps to keep you away from sin. Positive peer pressure occurs when true friends challenge each other to make wise choices. This kind of peer pressure helps you to be real and allows the light of Jesus Christ to shine in your life. The result will be that others can see the difference He makes in your life and they will want to know Him too.

When you make the right choice in the midst of peer pressure, you may find someone else willing to stand up alongside you because your courage helped that other person step forward. Some teens have been able to influence whole groups of kids to do the right thing, and the right choice ended up being the "cool" choice after all. It's all about leadership, and who will be the bold one willing to take the lead.

let's talk about it

1. Have you ever been pressured by "friends" to do things you knew were not right? How did you handle it?

2. Why do you think "friends" would try to get you to do something that they know is wrong?

   Suggested answer: One of the main things you want your daughter to discover with this question is: "Perhaps they are not really my friends." True friends would not encourage you to do something that is wrong, potentially harmful, or could get you into trouble. True friends love you without conditions, not just when you do the things they want you to do. True friends do not use each other for personal gain, such as to become more popular.

3. Have you ever given in to negative peer pressure? How did it make you feel? What were the results?

4. Have you ever taken a stand for what is right when pressured to do wrong? How did taking a stand for what is right make you feel? What were the results?

5. When you weigh the difference between how you felt and the results afterwards, which would you say is better: giving in or taking a stand?

TAKE THE PEER PRESSURE SURVEY!

Read each statement carefully. Write T next to the statements that are mostly true of your circle of friends and F next to the statements that are false.

_____1. My peers encourage me to treat others with kindness and respect.

_____2. My peers encourage me to dress in a way that will honor God, my family, and myself.

_____3. My peers honor and obey their parents and expect me to do the same.

_____4. My peers respect and follow school rules and expect me to do the same.

_____5. My peers encourage me to refrain from shoplifting and taking things that do not belong to me.

_____6. My peers do not use bad language and they expect me to do likewise.

_____7. My peers do not smoke, use drugs or alcohol, and they expect the same standards of me.

_____8. My peers have a close relationship with the Lord and encourage me to have the same.

_____9. My peers stand up for what is right and expect me to do the same.

_____10. My peers encourage me to remain pure in my relationships with guys.

My Heart Belongs to Him — My Identity

let's talk about it

1. What are the results of your Peer Pressure Survey? Did you have more true answers or more false answers?

2. What do your answers tell you about the kind of peer pressure you are receiving from your friends? What do your answers reveal to you about your friends?

3. What about you? What kind of peer pressure are you giving your friends? Are you pressuring them to do what is right? If not, why not?

4. What changes can you make in your life to improve the kind of peer pressure you are giving and receiving?

Tip:
Ask your daughter if she has ever seen positive peer pressure at work. If so, ask her to share some examples with you. Ask if she can see the benefits of positive peer pressure in the lives of any of her peers, or in her own life. If so, ask her to explain.

Truth, Dare, and Consequences

Always remember that with every choice there comes a consequence (an outcome or result). When you stand for truth and make good choices, you are rewarded with good consequences—some you may not see right away. But rest assured, you will be rewarded. On the flip side, when you take someone up on a dare, give in to negative peer pressure, or make bad choices, you are guaranteed to suffer bad consequences—you will pay a price. Often the price is much higher than you really want to pay.

Unfortunately, many young people do not consider the consequences when they are faced with tough choices. For example, many do not think about the real possibility of pregnancy or disease when they are thinking about giving in to premarital sex. And not many young people think about the possibility of endangering their health or becoming addicted and needing professional help when they are thinking about experimenting with drugs and alcohol. However, if you think about the consequences when you are facing negative peer pressure and consider the cost before you make a wrong choice, you will probably stand your ground and keep from giving in. Why? Because more than likely, you won't want to pay the price.

let's talk about it

What are the possible consequences of the following scenarios?

1. Debbie has a big test at school tomorrow. Her friends want her to go to a football game with them tonight, where they plan to sneak alcohol in and "party." Debbie wants to fit in with this crowd of popular kids, so she decides to accept their invitation.

My Heart Belongs to Him — My Identity

2. Rebecca wants to go to the movies tonight with a group of friends from school, but her parents would not approve of their choice of movies. Her friends encourage her to lie to her parents and tell them she is going to see a movie that they would approve of, in order to get permission to go. "They'll never know," they say. "We do it all the time." Rebecca gives in and decides to go with the flow.

3. Jackie wants to buy the latest style of designer jeans that everyone else is wearing, but her parents cannot afford to give her the money right away. Her friends suggest going to the mall to steal a pair. In desperation to fit in with the other girls, she decides to go for it.

let's pray about it

Talk to God and ask Him to give you the courage to take a stand for doing what is right, even when doing what is right is the unpopular choice. Ask Him to give you the wisdom to consider the consequences before making choices and the strength to challenge your friends to do the same.

STOP HERE! If you prefer to do this session in two parts, you may find this to be a natural place to stop. However, if you want to complete this session in one sitting, please continue.

get direction

As you interact with your peers from day to day, you will find yourself struggling to stand strong and do what's right.

You need to know that when kids pressure you to do things that are not right, they do not have your best interests at heart. They don't care that you might get hurt or what consequences you might have to pay. At that point the only thing they care about is themselves and their own need to fit in.

In the long run, you can gain more respect and approval from others if you dare to be different and take a bold stand for doing what is right. That's why it's important to have friends who share your values. You can be there for each other—to encourage and comfort one another when the going gets tough. It always feels good to know you have someone in your corner.

Remember that true Christian friends will challenge you to grow spiritually, to do good works, and to make right choices. You can challenge them in the same way. Throughout your teen years you will have to face negative peer pressure time and time again. Just remember that someone is always watching you, waiting for you to take a bold stand and lead the way to do what's right. God wants you to be that leader in your circle of friends.

BE STRONG IN THE LORD

Ephesians 6:10-11 says, "Finally, be strong in the Lord, and in the strength of His might. Put on the full armor of God, so that you will be able to stand firm against the schemes of the devil." Make a daily practice of becoming strong in the Lord. You can do this by spending time with Him every day, reading His Word, getting involved in your church, and by choosing your friends wisely. Make a commitment to spend time with friends who share your desire to do what's right and to please the Lord. Because you are a soldier in God's army, you must be equipped to do battle against evil at any time.

let's talk about it

1. Can you think of anything that you've ever done because everyone else was doing it? Share your experience. How did it make you feel? What were the consequences?

2. Read Proverbs 14:12. What does this verse say can happen to people who are doing what is right in their own eyes?

Suggested answer: Doing what is right in your own eyes rather than what is right according to the Word of God can lead to failure, problems, troubles, and even death. The Bible is our instruction book for putting our lives together. Trying to put life together without those necessary instructions will not work.

There is a way which seems right to a man, but its end is the way of death.

Proverbs 14:12

3. As a Christian, God has called you to go against the flow—to do what is right according to His Word, which sometimes involves great struggle. Read Ephesians 6:10-13. What has God given you to equip you for battle? Who is your battle really against when you are facing negative peer pressure and the temptation to make bad choices?

Suggested answer: God has given us His armor so that we will be able to protect ourselves from the strategies and tricks of Satan. We are not fighting against flesh and blood, but against Satan, his huge army of fallen angels, and the evil forces at work in our world.

4. Read Ephesians 6:14-17 (if possible, from *The Living Bible*), and list each piece of armor. How do you think each piece can help you?

Suggested answer: Here's how each piece of the armor can protect you:

a. **Strong Belt (Girdle) of Truth**—Standing for truth keeps you strong in your moral convictions (values and standards) and keeps your sense of integrity (honesty) in place. Confidence comes with certainty about the truthfulness of God's Word. Therefore, it is very important to know what the Bible says is true in every area of life.

b. **Breastplate of Righteousness**—God's approval. Righteousness refers to uprightness of character and loyalty to God's Word. Growing to be more and more like Him gives us confidence to resist temptation. We are protected by living out a righteous lifestyle as we yield to the Holy Spirit.

c. **Shoes** (that are able to speed you on as you preach the Good News of peace with God)—These help us as we walk through life and protect us through trials and temptations, just as the soldier's sandals protected him as he marched through thorns and thistles.

d. **The Shield of Faith**—Just as a soldier would be defenseless without his shield, we are defenseless without faith in God.

For I am confident of this very thing, that He who began a good work in you will perfect it until the day of Christ Jesus.

Philippians 1:6

e. **The Helmet of Salvation**—Knowing that God has saved us gives us hope of victory. The Christian's final ground of confidence is that God is faithful to complete the salvation He has begun (Philippians 1:6).

f. **Sword of the Spirit (Word of God)**—We cannot hope for victory unless we are armed with God's Word. We must study the Bible so we understand what truth is, and we should memorize passages of Scripture. Attempting to fight temptation without God's Word is like a soldier attempting to fight the enemy with his bare hands.

DON'T BE AFRAID TO TAKE A STAND

Standing up for what's right takes a lot of courage, especially when you have to stand alone. It is because of fear that many young people and adults alike give in to negative peer pressure. There are many things they may be afraid of, such as being excluded from the "in-crowd" or losing a friendship. Whatever the reason, fear can cause you to make bad choices that you will regret later. Because of the fear of suffering for doing what is right, you may have to suffer much more for doing what is wrong. 1 Peter 3:17 says, "For it is better, if God should will it so, that you suffer for doing what is right rather than for doing what is wrong."

Fear is one of the Christian's greatest enemies. Fear can actually control your life if you allow it to. However, when Jesus is Lord of your life, He is the only One who should have full control of your life. God's Word should guide your choices, not fear. Fear can keep you from being all that God wants you to be. It can hinder you from making right choices, and it can cripple you at times when you need to lead the way for others.

Tip:

Share the following example to illustrate 1 Peter 3:17. If a group of friends decides to shoplift while at the mall, you can choose to do one of two things. Either you can say no and refuse to participate (which would involve walking away and perhaps even calling Mom or Dad to pick you up) or you can give in to the negative peer pressure and choose to participate in shoplifting. If you choose the first option, you may suffer by having your friends call you a chicken, tease you, and even ridicule you. However, if you choose the second option, you may suffer by getting caught and having to face the humiliation of all of the consequences that go along with shoplifting (possible time in a juvenile detention center, punishment from parents, loss of a good reputation, and so on). And if you don't get caught, you may suffer from the agonizing guilt of knowing what you did was wrong.

Wouldn't you rather suffer for doing what was right? You may even be rewarded later for making the right choice. For example, God may bless you with the very thing the girls were proposing to steal. You will certainly receive other spiritual blessings, such as peace and joy, as a result of doing the right thing before the Lord. What's more, you may even convince the girls to follow you in doing what is right!

let's talk about it

1. What are some reasons why Christian teens might be afraid to stand up for what's right when faced with negative peer pressure?

Suggested answer: They may be afraid of being excluded from the "in-crowd," or thought of as weird or different. They may be afraid of offending their peers, or of losing a friendship. Or they may be afraid of being teased, laughed at, or losing popularity.

2. Can you remember a time when you were afraid to take a stand when you were being pressured to do something you knew was wrong? What were you afraid of? Share your experience.

3. What do the following verses have to say about fear?

a. Psalm 27:1-3

Suggested answer: We don't need to fear because God protects us, comes to our defense, and gives us victory.

b. Psalm 34:4

Suggested answer: We can trust God to take away all of our fears.

c. Isaiah 41:10

Suggested answer: We don't have to be afraid or anxious about anything because God is always with us. He gives us His strength and courage to make right choices.

4. What are some ways that you can use God's Word to guide your choices?

Suggested answer: Whenever you are pressured to do something, ask yourself first what God's Word has to say about it. If it is against His Word, you should not do it. If you are afraid of what others might think or say, pray and ask God for His strength to overcome that fear, and follow His Word. When you do this, you are allowing God's Word to guide your choices, not fear.

5. Read 2 Timothy 1:7, then personalize it by rewriting it here, inserting "me" in place of "us." Commit this verse to memory this week.

get going

When someone is encouraging you to do something that might lead to trouble, use the following steps to help you make a wise choice and to stand for what is right.

This is the life application section of the session. It includes practical guidelines and action points to help your daughter live out what she has learned.

FOUR STEPS TO OVERCOMING NEGATIVE PEER PRESSURE

1. **Think through the consequences.**
    - Is it against God's Word or against the law?
    - Will it be harmful to me or to others (physically, emotionally, or spiritually)?
    - Will it disappoint God, my family, or others?
    - Would I be hurt or upset if someone did this to me?
    - Will I be sorry afterward?
    - What could be the consequences of making this choice?

My Heart Belongs to Him — My Identity

If you can answer yes to any of the first five questions, your response to the pressure to join in should be "NO."

2. **Know what you stand for and refuse to give in.**

Like the saying goes, "If you don't stand for something, you'll fall for anything." Know what your convictions are. Set standards for yourself that you are committed to live by.

For example, if you have set the standard for yourself to wait until marriage to have sex, be committed to live by that standard. That way, when you are pressured to give in to premarital sex, you can take a bold stand for your values and convictions and say, "No! That goes against the standards that I have set for myself." You may run the risk of sounding as if you're scared or boring, or too religious—but you will save yourself from serious consequences, and a lot of heartache and pain in the long run.

3. **Know positive options and suggest alternatives.**

Maybe you can suggest a better activity—something more positive, safe, and moral. Hebrews 10:24 says, "And let us consider how to stimulate one another to love and good deeds." There may be at least one other person who feels like you do but is afraid to say something. If you make a suggestion, he or she will probably support you. However, after you have taken a stand for your values and beliefs, if the others still want to make a wrong choice, that is your cue to walk away. Look for God's way of escape (1 Corinthians 10:13) and take it!

4. **Turn over the situation to God.**

The Bible says in James 4:7-8, "Submit therefore to God. Resist the devil and he will flee from you. Draw near to God and He will draw near to you." Whenever you are facing negative peer pressure or the temptation to do wrong, turn the situation over to God. Submit yourself to Him in obedience and refuse to give in, and as God's Word promises, the devil will run away from you.

Tip:
Believe it or not, by the time they are in the sixth grade, most girls have already made some decisions about how far they will go physically with guys. Challenge your daughter in the critical area of dating and courtship decision-making before she begins the process. Share with her the importance of a holy standard in relationships with members of the opposite sex. Discuss how far she will go. Don't force your views at this point, but take the time to share your values and boundaries. Then, invite her to think about this and accept your convictions as her own. Help her draw those lines.

Warning! Avoid discussing your own significant moral failures with your child, especially in the area of sex. Adolescents need role models, not an excuse to sin.

No temptation has overtaken you that is not common to man; and God is faithful, who will not allow you to be tempted beyond what you are able, but with the temptation will provide the way of escape also, so that you will be able endure it.
1 Corinthians 10:13

Tip For Taking God's Way of Escape:

Here is a biblical example that you might want to share with your daughter—Joseph and Potiphar's wife. If time allows, you can read the biblical account in Genesis 39:1-13. If not, you can share the following from that passage.

While serving in Potiphar's house, Joseph was confronted several times by Potiphar's wife with negative peer pressure. She constantly pressured Joseph to sin with her sexually. But each time, Joseph said no! He refused. When it became intense, Joseph asked an important question, "How can I do this great wickedness and sin against God?" He acknowledged that it was wrong, and he acknowledged that he would be sinning against God, who had been loving and faithful toward him. When she continued to pressure him, in spite of his refusals, he knew it was his cue to leave. The Bible says he "fled," which means that not only did he leave, he ran away quickly! And not only did he run from her, he actually ran away from the house!

Will you follow Joseph's example and run from sin when necessary? Look for God's escape—and take it!

 let's talk about it

Take a look at the following scenarios and discuss how you can stand for what is right in each situation. Use the four steps that you just learned to deal with the negative peer pressure presented in each case.

1. Some friends want you to sneak around your parents and come over tonight while your mom and dad are not at home. How would you handle their pressure?

2. A friend has the same math class as you, but at a different time of day. She received her test score back and it was 100 percent. She reveals to you that she cheated, and she offers you her test paper to study the answers before you take the test later on in the day. What would you do?

3. While at a sleepover at a friend's house, one of the girls sneaks in some alcohol. After the parents have gone to bed, everyone is going to drink some, and now it's your turn.

What Happens If I Fall?

You may be asking yourself, "What happens if I give in to the pressure and make an unwise choice? Will I be doomed? Will God still love me? Will there still be hope for me?" Always remember that God is a loving, merciful God, full of grace and ready to forgive. Though you will have consequences to pay when you make wrong choices, God will forgive you. He can also rescue you from whatever is causing you to stumble, if you will trust Him and submit yourself and the situation to Him.

Forgiveness involves first confessing your sin to God (see David's example in Psalm 32:1-7). Once we confess our sins to God, 1 John 1:9 tells us that God is faithful to forgive us our sins and to cleanse us from all unrighteousness. So not only will God forgive you, He will also give you a clean slate.

Second, you must repent, which means to turn away from the sin and toward God. This may mean distancing yourself from the person or activity associated with the temptation that led you to sin, until you are strong enough to take a bold stand against that temptation.

Third, as a part of repentance you will need to make a sincere commitment to God not to willfully sin in that way again. And finally, you should pray daily for God's strength and for the power and guidance of the Holy Spirit as you walk out your commitment. So remember if you fall, don't lose hope ... get up again and go forward with God's help!

> *... God is light, and in Him there is no darkness at all. If we say that we have fellowship with Him and yet walk in darkness, we lie and do not practice the truth.*
>
> 1 John 1: 5b-6

> *If we confess our sins, He is faithful and righteous to forgive us our sins and to cleanse us from all unrighteousness.*
>
> 1 John 1:9

let's pray about it

Talk to God and ask Him to help you remember the four important steps to help you stand strong whenever you face negative peer pressure. Ask Him to help you as you develop your convictions (values and standards) and to give you the wisdom, strength, and courage to live by them.

POINT OF DISCOVERY

Here your daughter will record the key principles that she has learned in this session (those truths that stood out to her the most). If your daughter needs help, feel free to offer suggestions.

Here's what I discovered in this session:

PERSONAL ACTION STEPS

Your daughter will record the personal changes she plans to make in her life as a result of what she has learned. Again, feel free to offer suggestions if she needs help.

NOTE: Have your daughter select one or two action points that she most wants to apply, and then have her write it (them) on the Personal Action Steps sheet on page 3 of her book.

Because my heart belongs to Him, I will:

keep moving

Over the next week, take some time to think through (and then write out) your standards. What will you stand for? What will you not stand for (tolerate or participate in)? You should have standards regarding how you will treat others, time spent with guys, habits (such as drinking, drugs, cigarettes), cheating, choosing friends, dress, language, media you look at or listen to, lying, your attitude, busyness, settling for "good enough," your appearance, and responsibility.

Here are some guidelines for writing your standards:

- Use first person: "I will ..." or "I will not ..."

- Make them action oriented.

- Make them specific.

- Use Bible verses as your guidelines.
  Example: Because 1 Corinthians 6:18a says to flee from sexual immorality, I will not participate in any sexual activity before marriage.

- Be realistic (do not overcommit yourself).
  Example: Do not commit to spend time alone with God in prayer three times a day for one hour each time, if you know realistically you will only pray twice a day for fifteen minutes. (Do not make commitments you cannot keep).

This section features additional projects. They are designed to help your daughter deepen her experience, and to encourage you to participate in her growth process. Feel free to use one or more of the assignments or projects presented, or use your creativity to create one or two of your own.

A Special Note to Mom:

From time to time, ask your daughter how she is doing with keeping her standards. Go over her list of standards with her at least once a quarter, and help her evaluate herself in light of the standards she has set for herself. Ask questions like: *Are you having trouble following the standards you have set for yourself? If yes, why? What things in your life do you think you may need to change to help you honor God's standards? Is there anything I can do to help you in keeping your standards? What convictions (values) have you had to stand up for recently? How did you do? How did you feel? What difference did your taking a stand make? What was the result of not taking a stand? Do you feel you need to raise or lower any of your standards? Why or why not?*

Session 6

The Importance of Guarding My Purity

*Or do you not know that
your body is a temple of the Holy Spirit,
who is in you,
whom you have received from God?
You are not your own;
you were bought at a price.
Therefore honor God with your body.*
1 Corinthians 6:19 (NIV)

Reflection

To review the previous session and to follow up on projects and assignments, ask your daughter the following four questions:

1. Thinking back over the previous session, what life-changing truth would you say stood out most to you?

2. How are you doing on your "Personal Action Steps" from the last session?

3. What progress have you made with your "Keep Moving" assignments and/or projects from the previous session? (Be sure to encourage her to complete those assignments or projects that she has not yet completed.)

4. Is there anything else from the previous session that you would like to talk about?

Focus

God wants you to live a pure and holy life morally, emotionally, and physically. There are consequences when you don't live life this way, and incredible benefits when you do.

OBJECTIVES:

You will help your daughter understand the importance of guarding her purity as you guide her to:

- Understand the basic dynamics of puberty and sexual maturity.

- Recognize the sexual pressure that society puts on young people through today's music, TV programs, movies, and other cultural forces.

- Become aware of the false teachings regarding "safe sex."

- Discover what God's Word has to say about the importance of guarding her purity.

- Learn practical ways to guard her purity—morally, emotionally, and physically.

- Consider the consequences of not guarding her physical purity and the benefits of choosing to wait.

- Discover the answer to the question, "Is it too late for me?" for those who have not guarded their purity.

get ready

A PRICELESS GIFT

This section features a fictional story and related discussion questions. It introduces your daughter to the topic and sparks an interest in the material to be covered in this session. Read the story aloud together, then discuss the questions.

One evening when Haley came home from youth night she asked her mom if they could talk about that night's lesson, which was about love, sex, and dating. Haley loved to have "girl talks" with her mom. She especially loved to hear her mother's stories about when she was younger. They talked for what seemed like hours about boys, love, and dating. Then finally the tone of the conversation became more serious as Haley's mom began to explain the importance of remaining pure until marriage.

"Your physical purity is a precious treasure," said Haley's mom, " … a priceless gift. God desires that you cherish that gift until you get married. It's a gift that He wants you to give only to your husband—the one who will be committed to you and who will cherish and protect you for life."

"Did you save your gift for Dad until you got married?" Haley asked with curiosity.

"Oh, yes, Honey, I did! And what an honor it was to be able to give your dad—the man who committed to love me for a lifetime—such a priceless gift on our wedding night." Haley smiled. "And by the way," her mom continued, "it was such an honor and a blessing to receive the same gift from him in return. It was the best wedding gift we could give each other."

"Wow," said Haley with dreamy eyes. "That's so romantic."

"Yes, it was," said her mother smiling as she reminisced. Then after a brief pause she said, "But I'm sorry to say that many young women choose not to wait until marriage and make the mistake of giving away their gift too soon." Haley's eyes widened as her mother continued. "When a young woman becomes emotionally involved with a guy she may believe that she is in love with him. Oftentimes, when you give away your heart, your body will soon follow. Unfortunately, many young women find that after becoming physically involved the relationship is never the same after that."

"What do you mean?" Haley asked inquisitively.

"Well usually the first thing she will experience is guilt. Because premarital sex is sin, the feelings of guilt are inescapable. She may feel guilty about letting God down, letting her parents down, and about letting herself down. In addition to guilt, worry is often felt, because there are possible consequences that come along with sexual sin."

"Well, I know you can become pregnant, or get an awful disease, but what other consequences can there be?" Haley asked.

"For one thing physical involvement can become the focus of the relationship, and when that happens, she may realize that he didn't really love her after all, leaving her heartbroken and feeling very much betrayed and alone."

"That sounds so sad," said Haley, "and I can understand how that can happen. You know how Dad often warns us that some guys are only after one thing? Now I see what he means."

"Yes, but unfortunately those guys don't understand that God's will for us to remain pure until marriage applies to both girls and guys. When a guy becomes physically involved before marriage, he too must face the consequences of sin and disobedience; not to mention that he is robbing his future wife of the most precious gift that he could give her … his purity."

"Wow, I never thought of it that way," said Haley in amazement.

"In addition to the other consequences I mentioned, a young woman can lose her good reputation and the respect of others when the news of her physical involvement gets around, and it often does."

"I know that's true," said Haley. "I've heard rumors at school. And it seems to really hurt those who the rumors are about."

"Yes, and for some young women, losing the respect of others and gaining a negative reputation in this way may cause them to lose respect for themselves. They may begin to feel worthless, and turn to a life of sexual promiscuity, which can bring about a lifetime of problems, heartache and pain. Then there are the feelings of regret, wishing that they could turn back the hands of time and undo what was done."

"It doesn't sound like there are any benefits whatsoever to premarital sex, and yet there is so much pressure out there to get physically involved. It doesn't seem to me to be worth the trouble. It just seems to create a lot of problems and pain," Haley observed.

"You see, Haley," her mom continued, "every person is given only one 'first time.' Once you lose your physical purity, you can never, ever get it back. But if you save that first time for your husband, what a precious wedding gift you can give him, and what a wonderful way to be able to honor God! If you really love someone you will wait, and he will wait for you. That's true love." Then looking Haley straight in the eyes, she said, "God wants that for you, Haley."

"I want that too, and I know that's what's best for me. But how do I know that someday I won't be faced with the pressure or even the desire to give in? What can I do to guard my purity and protect my gift?"

Warning!

As you discuss this story with your daughter, she will no doubt want to know how you did in the area of purity. Depending upon your experience, this could be a difficult discussion. Past failures must not prevent us from calling our children to God's standard. Avoid discussing significant moral failures with your child, especially in the area of sex. It's better if children do not know about moral failures of their parents when they are young. Continue to hold up a high standard and don't be a stumbling block (see Romans 14:13b).

Adolescents need role models, not an excuse to sin. Rather than share any details about significant past moral failures, we suggest you say something like this: "I didn't always make the best choices. It would have been easier if there had been a study like this to help me understand God's standards and to give me ways to live them out. My goal is to help you to live with full moral, emotional, and physical purity." If she presses, tell her that you might someday talk more with her when she's an adult, but that you don't want to discuss this any further at this time.

let's talk about it

1. What did Haley learn from her "girl talk" with her mom?

2. What would you say are some reasons why many of today's young people choose not to wait to have sex until marriage?

3. How would you answer Haley's last question? What would you say she could do to guard her purity and protect her gift?

My Heart Belongs to Him — My Identity

The teenage years are when a young person becomes sexually mature. This period of time is called puberty, and it usually begins around age twelve. If you are twelve or older, you are in the midst of a time when you are physically able to become pregnant and give birth to a child.

There is a strong flood of sexual hormones active in the body during your teenage years. This is a time of confusion, curiosity, fear, and excitement. Everything in your body is preparing for sexual activity, and the desire is strong. But before you mature to the adult years, you are not emotionally or financially able to handle the responsibilities and possible consequences that come with sexual activity. And if you are not married, you are not morally or spiritually ready.

Far too many young people are giving in to the pressure to have premarital sex. The message that society is giving youth through today's music, television programs, and movies about sex, love, and romance, is this: "If it feels good, do it. Do it as often as you want to and with as many people as you want to. Love has very little to do with sex, and marriage has almost nothing to do with sex. No rules! No limits! Just do it!" The message is that something is wrong with you if you are not involved physically—after all, everybody else is doing it! And every day, young people all over America are buying in to this message. Unfortunately, very little is said about the consequences of premarital sex.

Here are some statistics to give you an idea of how many teenagers are sexually active across America:

- Some studies indicate three-fourths of all girls had sex during their teenage years and 15% have had four or more partners. [1]

- More than one million teenage girls in the United States become pregnant each year. Of those who give birth, nearly half are not yet 18. [2]

- More than 400,000 teenage girls now have abortions each year. [3]

- Fifty six million Americans—many of them very young—are suffering from incurable, sexually transmitted viruses. [4]

- Teenagers are the fastest-rising age group for HIV infection. [5]

This section gives an overview of the topic. It gives your daughter "the big picture" as it is in our world today; for example "this is what's happening out there—this is what young women are facing." It will help your daughter relate to the topic on a personal level.

You may want to share with your daughter that in addition to the consequences of premarital sex, you also have to live with what you have done for the rest of your life. Even after marriage, if you marry, you will still have to deal with the baggage from those premarital relationships. Here are a few examples. (1) You may carry guilt that will negatively affect intimacy with your husband. (2) After learning of your past, your husband may not easily trust you, or respect you as much as he once did, and your past may be a constant issue between you. (3) You may have brought a child into your marriage (as a result of that premarital relationship). (4) You may have contracted a sexually transmitted disease (there are sexually transmitted diseases that have no cures, such as herpes, HIV, and AIDS) that causes problems in your marriage. (5) Because of a sexually transmitted disease called HPV (human papillomavirus), which can cause sterilization in women, you may not ever be able to have children. That consequence can be devastating to your life and relationship with your future husband.

WHAT IS "SAFE SEX"?

The only real "safe sex" is "no sex" until marriage, because that's the way God designed it. Nothing done apart from Him is safe. Sex outside of marriage can even be life threatening. Many people have died and are dying every day from the AIDS virus, and yet thousands of young people continue to take that risk every day. They make the mistake of thinking, *Oh, that wouldn't happen to me.* They believe that all they have to do is practice "safe sex" and they will be protected. The truth is, condoms are **not** 100% effective at protecting you from pregnancy or from disease. In his book entitled *Life on the Edge*, Dr. James Dobson explains that there are viruses small enough to penetrate the latex rubber of a condom. HIV and HPV (human papillomavirus) are such viruses. HPV is a disease that can cause many painful symptoms and sterilization in women!

In studies conducted at the University of Texas Medical Branch at Galveston, researchers concluded that condoms were only 69% effective in preventing the transmission of HIV. That means there is a 31% chance that a person can contract AIDS while using a condom—not very good odds. [6]

Emotional and sexual intimacy before marriage is in direct disobedience to God's Word. With disobedience, there are consequences to pay, such as feeling separated from God, guilt, heartache, regrets, possibly a sexually transmitted disease (including AIDS), pregnancy, abortion, a bad reputation, and the loss of virginity, which was meant to be saved as a special gift for your husband.

let's talk about it

1. Are the statistics regarding the sexual activity of teenagers surprising to you? Why or why not?

2. What do you think are some of the consequences of premarital sex (list as many as you can)? How can those consequences change a person's life?

Suggested answer: A few of the consequences are separation from God, guilt, heartache, regrets, loss of virginity, loss of a good reputation, pregnancy, abortion, sexually transmitted diseases including AIDS, and possible death.

3. Do you think that most young people consider the consequences of premarital sex before getting involved sexually? Why do you think so many teenagers are involved in sexual relationships in spite of the risks and possible consequences of sex before marriage?

Suggested answer: Some reasons include peer pressure, today's cultural influences (to wait until marriage to have sex is old fashioned), to meet their emotional needs for love and affection, to prove their love to the other person, and to hold on to the other person. Also, most teens think that they are invincible. They think nothing bad could happen to them, so they easily shrug off the possible consequences.

4. Do you know anyone who has had to suffer the consequences of premarital sex? What have you learned from their experiences?

5. Is the threat of pregnancy and getting sexually transmitted diseases (including AIDS) the most important reason why a person who is not married should not have sex?

Suggested answer: No, the most important reason why an unmarried person should not have sex is because God forbids it. He forbids it because it is so dangerous to you mentally, emotionally, and spiritually. The Bible says that the sin of immorality is a unique sin that hurts you personally and deeply. Premarital sex will also create many problems for you in your future marriage and rob your of the incredible blessings that saving yourself for marriage will bring.

Flee immorality. Every other sin that a man commits is outside the body, but the immoral man sins against his own body.

1 Corinthians 6:18

Session 6 — The Importance of Guarding My Purity

The Silver Box [7]

By Nathan Scholl (at age 19)

Shining, it rests on my warm hands.

Its luster beams out in tiny strands.

Silver is the color of purity,

A box is the symbol of treasure.

My hands tremble, my fingers shake.

Lord, may I not open this box you have given me.

I press it close to my heart wanting to set its contents free.

Though I cannot see, what the future may hold.

I will not pry the lid; I will not try to unfold.

This silver box ... so pure.

So Lord give me patience,

And Lord I pray I may be secure.

That what I wait for this day

Is a treasure worth infinitely more than what I endure.

My Heart Belongs to Him — My Identity

get direction

God created sex, and it is nothing to be ashamed of. He has a special plan for sex. He made sex so that we can bring new babies into our families. He also made sex to be pleasurable and fun—for us to enjoy within the commitment of marriage. In those circumstances, it is something for us to feel good and not guilty about.

The wonder and enjoyment of this intimacy is greatly enhanced through remaining pure until marriage. He has the best in mind for us, and He makes it clear that we should not experience emotional or sexual intimacy with a man before marriage.

This section provides a clear picture of what the Bible has to say about this topic. The biblical truths and principles examined in this section will help your daughter apply God's Word to her life.

let's talk about it

1. Read Psalm 42:1-2. Who does this verse say we should long for, and deeply desire to spend time with? According to Colossians 3:1-4, what should you have your mind and affections set on? Are your affections in the right place?

   Suggested answer: You should long for and want to spend time with God, as much as a deer pants for water when it is thirsty. Your mind and your affections should be set on heavenly things where Christ is seated at the right hand of God, not on earthly things. As a Christian, your life is hidden in Him—He is your life.

2. What do the following verses say about sexual immorality? (Note: "Immorality" means sin, evil, or corruption.)

   Colossians 3:5

   Suggested answer: This verse says that you should do away with all sinful things and put to death all sinful desires that are within you. In addition, it says that you should have nothing to do with sexual immorality, impurity, lust, or shameful desires.

   1 Corinthians 6:18-20

   Suggested answer: This passage says that you should run from sexual sin, and that no other sin affects the body like this sin. It also says when you sin sexually it is a sin against your own body, which is

Put to death, therefore, whatever belongs to your earthly nature: sexual immorality, impurity, lust, evil desires and greed, which is idolatry.
Colossians 3:5 (NIV)

the home of the Holy Spirit who lives within you. In addition, this passage reminds you that as a Christian, your body does not belong to you, but to God who bought you with a great price—the death of His only begotten Son, Jesus.

1 Thessalonians 4:3-8

Suggested answer: This passage says that it is God's will for you to stay away from all sexual sin, and that you should control your body in a way that is holy and honorable, not in lustful passion like those who do not know Him. It warns that God will greatly punish those who sin in this way (fornication: sex outside of marriage, and adultery: sexual unfaithfulness of a married person). This passage also reminds you that God did not call you to impure thoughts (dirty-minded and full of lust), but to live a holy life. Whoever disobeys or rejects these rules is disobeying or rejecting God, not man.

Ephesians 5:3-10

Suggested answer: According to this passage, there should not even be a hint of sexual immorality or any other impurity among Christians, because these things are improper for God's holy people. Because of God's light within you, you should do only what is good, and right, and true.

3. How can you honor God with your body as stated in 1 Corinthians 6:20?

Suggested answer: You can honor God with your body by using every part of it to give glory to God. This would mean making right choices and exercising good moral values in your life. This would also mean refusing to use your body for anything that is evil or sinful (anything that is against God's Word).

4. What do you think is meant in Ephesians 5:3 by "not even a hint" of sexual immorality or any kind of impurity?

Suggested answer: It means that you should avoid even the slightest suggestion or whisper of sexual immorality or impurity. Don't allow yourself to even toy with thoughts in this area. Instead take every thought captive and make it obedient to Christ (see 2 Corinthians 10:5).

According to God's Word and will for our lives, our goal morally, emotionally, and physically must be … purity. When most people think of purity, the first thing that comes to mind is physical purity or virginity. It's true that physical purity is very important, and God intends for you to reserve your physical purity until marriage. It's not because He's old-fashioned or trying to rob you of having fun, but because He loves you and wants to protect you from harm and from a broken heart. However, there is much more to purity than virginity. God wants you to live a pure and holy life, morally and emotionally, as well as physically (sexually).

STOP HERE! If you prefer to do this session in two parts, you may find this to be a natural place to stop. However, if you want to complete this session in one sitting, please continue.

GUARDING YOUR MORAL PURITY

Guarding your moral purity (your heart and mind) involves knowing the difference between right and wrong and choosing to do right according to God's Word. It comes as a result of developing a Christ-like character. For example, if you are thinking *right thoughts* and being influenced by the *right things* (the Bible and wholesome books, television programs, movies, and music) and the *right people* (parents, godly teachers, counselors, and Christian friends), your feelings for others will be pure, which will help you to keep your actions pure. However, if you allow sexual images and messages to influence your heart and mind, your moral purity will be unprotected and you will more than likely begin to have impure feelings, which you will eventually want to experience physically. As you can see, your moral purity helps to guard your emotional and physical purity. It all starts with a heart that belongs to Him.

let's talk about it

1. What would you say are some ways that you can guard your moral purity?

Suggested answer: You can make wise entertainment choices, choose your friends wisely, read God's Word often, pray, spend time with other Christians, choose wholesome activities, and so on. You also need to work to take every thought captive according to 2 Corinthians 10:5.

Tip:

You may want to share with your daughter that many girls think that having a boyfriend is one of the most important things in life, and it becomes their focus. It's all they think about, talk about, and dream about. Sadly, many girls think that having a one-on-one relationship with a boy will make them happy and complete. However, the truth is, no man, woman, or child can fill her deepest desires. They can only be fulfilled through Jesus Christ, and only He can truly meet her needs. Colossians 2:9,10 says, "For in Him all the fullness of Deity dwells in bodily form, and in Him you have been made complete, and He is the head over all rule and authority." There is nothing in life that can complete us—not friends, or popularity, or clothes, or a boyfriend, or anything else. The only way we can be complete is by having a growing relationship with Jesus. In the Living Bible, Colossians 2:10a says, *"So you have everything when you have Christ … ."*

2. How does God's Word in Psalm 119:9-11 say that young men or young women can keep themselves pure?

Suggested answer: We can keep ourselves pure by living our lives according to God's Word.

3. Read Philippians 4:8-9. What guidelines does this passage of Scripture give us for making good decisions to protect our moral purity? How should this affect the way you live?

Suggested answer: Philippians 4:8-9 tells us that we should only allow those things that are true, honorable, right, pure, lovely, of good repute, portraying excellence, or worthy of praise to enter our hearts and minds. Therefore, if any of your friendships, music, movies, TV programs, or activities are not true, honorable, right, pure, lovely, or of good repute—portraying excellence, or worthy of praise—they are not for you and can compromise your moral purity.

GUARDING YOUR EMOTIONAL PURITY

Emotional purity involves keeping your feelings pure, which helps to keep you from becoming emotionally attached to someone of the opposite sex prematurely (before it is time). It is both wrong and dangerous to build exclusive attachments to a young man until you're ready to get married. Your affections should be set on the Lord at this time in your life, and you should long for Him. 2 Corinthians 7:1 (TLB) says, "… Let us turn away from everything wrong, whether of body or spirit, and purify ourselves, living in the wholesome fear of God, giving ourselves to Him alone." Expressing emotional attachment (or a romantic love and loyalty) to a young man prematurely is like living out one of the privileges of marriage without being married. The danger of this kind of commitment to a young man is that emotional intimacy tends to quickly move a relationship toward physical intimacy. In addition, shouldn't you save this exclusive emotional attachment for your future husband? Should he just be another guy in a long line of guys that you attached yourself to?

As you grow and mature into a woman of God, you should focus on building friendships with guys, not romance. Always remember that your heart and your emotions often lead your body. A heart surrendered to God leads your emotions and your body down the paths of righteousness.

Proverbs 4:23 (NIV) says, "Above all else, guard your heart, for it is the wellspring of life."

GUARDING YOUR PHYSICAL PURITY

God gave you the incredible gift of innocence and purity. This wonderful gift is one that you should treasure and protect so that you can present this gift to your husband on your wedding night. How much of your innocence do you want to save to give to your future husband? How much of your innocence do you want to give away to other young men that are not your husband? It is best for you to avoid situations that can tempt you sexually, such as being alone with someone of the opposite sex in private unsupervised places, or for long lengths of time. The Bible gives you a great guide: "Abstain from all appearance of evil." (1 Thessalonians 5:22 KJV). It is not good to involve yourself in sexual activities, such as kissing, making out or heavy petting, because such activities cause you to become sexually aroused. These physical activities could lead to intercourse. The body only knows how to read the feelings that come from those activities, and you will want to continue experiencing the pleasure until satisfied. Once you allow your body to experience those feelings, it is hard to control or deny your body. How much sexual feeling should you be sharing with a man who is not your husband? None! You are giving away some of that gift of purity to a guy who should not have it. The "just say no!" approach that our culture suggests is very tough to follow, unless you remember that the ability to guide your body to do what is right (guarding your physical purity) starts with guarding your moral and emotional purity.

Above all else, guard your heart, for it is the wellspring of life.
Proverbs 4:23 (NIV)

Tip:
Reassure your daughter that it is possible to live a pure life in an impure world, but that it is an awesome challenge. God has provided a way for her to meet that challenge. 1 Corinthians 10:13 says, "No temptation has overtaken you but such as is common to man; and God is faithful, who will not allow you to be tempted beyond what you are able, but with the temptation will provide the way of escape also, so that you will be able to endure it." This verse tells us that you will not come up against any temptation that others have not already experienced, or that is too much for you to bear. In addition, when you do experience temptation, God will provide a way out for you so that you can stand true to your values and to His Word and will for your life. What is the way out that He will provide? His wisdom to know the difference between right and wrong, His courage to make the right choice and say no, and His strength to walk away—even in the midst of great pressure. For more information on ways to escape temptation see "Four Steps to Overcoming Negative Peer Pressure" in Session 5.

CAUTION: INTIMACY IS MEANT TO PROGRESS!

It is good for a man not to touch a woman.

I Corinthians 7:1b

Physical intimacy was created for marriage. Therefore it was meant to progress, and it can be very powerful. You can see how intimacy progresses in the lives of people, maybe even people you know. (Nancy writing:) My daughter Sarah, in a talk to a class of sixth graders, put it this way: "When you are going out with a guy, one of the first signs of affection is touch. Soon there is a desire for more, so he begins holding your hand—heading your friendship toward romance. Before long, you notice that all your friends are doing so much more with their boyfriends, and besides, just holding hands doesn't satisfy you anymore. So you decide to begin kissing, which ignites the passion. By this time you are becoming emotionally attached, isolating yourself from friends and family. Many at this point begin to experiment with making out and heavy petting, which prepares the body for and can even lead to sexual intercourse. The two then begin to experience an attachment to each other that was only intended for marriage."

let's talk about it

1. What do you think a friendship with a guy would look like without any physical involvement? How would you define physical involvement?

Suggested answer: A friendship without physical involvement would be one that is built and shared only in group settings. The conversation would be brief and light; you wouldn't share your soul with each other, and touch would be very limited. Physical involvement can be defined as touch leading toward intimacy, such as holding hands, hugging, kissing, petting, and sexual intercourse.

2. Do you think that it's possible to stay away from romantic relationships with guys? Why or why not?

Suggested answer: It is possible to stay away from romantic relationships with guys, but you have to be very disciplined in how you build your relationship, and you must both have an understanding of the purpose and the benefits of building a friendship instead of a romance. You must also both agree that you should spend little or no one-on-one time together because it breeds intimacy.

My Heart Belongs to Him — My Identity

3. Have you made a decision to abstain (do without, stay away) from sex until marriage? Why or why not? How has your decision affected your life and those around you?

4. Where do your friends stand regarding these issues? Where would you say most teens draw the line in terms of how far they'll go with the opposite sex (being alone with the opposite sex, holding hands, kissing, touching body parts, passionate hugging and kissing, lying down and making out, removing clothes, intercourse)?

5. In what ways do you agree or disagree with them? Where do you want to draw the line?

Tip:
You should mention to your daughter that some people advocate the concept of the "wedding kiss." This concept says that in order to take every precaution in protecting your purity, you should save your first kiss for your husband on your wedding day. Challenge your daughter to consider this bold stand for purity. If it sounds too radical for her, ask her where she will draw the line and how much of her innocence she plans to give away to guys who have no right to it.

BENEFITS OF GUARDING YOUR PURITY

Is it easy to remain morally, emotionally, and physically pure? No. Is it worth it? Absolutely!! There are so many benefits to guarding your purity. The first and most important benefit is that it keeps your relationship right with the Lord and results in His abundant blessing. When you guard your purity in your relationships, you are able to build a reputation of honor and virtue that helps to strengthen your self-esteem. You avoid the emotional roller coaster of the going out, then breaking up dating scene. You escape all of the negative consequences associated with premarital sex. Also, focusing

If you are leading a girl through this study who is not your daughter, and you suspect that one or both of her parents is abusing her (emotionally, physically or sexually), you must act on her behalf. Let her know what you suspect and that you plan to discuss this with your pastor and the legal authorities so that they can investigate. The girl will not want this reported to anyone, but if you have reason to suspect abuse, it is important to follow through for her current safety and future well-being.

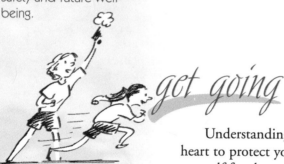

This is the life application section of the session. It includes practical guidelines and action points to help your daughter live out what she has learned.

on building friendships with guys rather than physical relationships will help your relationships with guys grow and mature in healthy ways.

In addition to presenting your husband with one of the best gifts you can give him when you get married, you will also be going into marriage with an atmosphere of trust, as you and your husband know that you reserved your emotional and physical purity for each other. What's more, your moral and emotional purity, plus your love for God, will help you remain faithful to each other once you are married. Then you will have an honorable testimony to share with your future children when you challenge them to purity.

get going

Understanding God's purpose for purity, and His role in guarding your heart to protect your purity, can give you hope and the ability to save yourself for the treasures He has in store for you. What a perfect gift to give your husband! What a wonderful way to honor God!

MORE WAYS TO GUARD YOUR PURITY

1. **Pray!**

Ask God to keep you mindful of the fact that your heart belongs to Him. Pray before entering into friendships with guys, and pray before spending time with guys. Ask the Lord to guide your thoughts and actions so that you do not encourage any young man romantically, but rather encourage him in his love for the Lord.

2. **Avoid discipleship relationships with guys.**

These relationships naturally become intimate because you share your innermost thoughts, feelings, and struggles. This closeness draws you together emotionally. Remember: Allow guys to disciple guys and girls to disciple girls.

3. **Set your standards and live by them.**

Make your choices about what you will or will not do with a guy, before spending time with him. Here are some helpful hints:

- Remember not to spend time alone with a guy.
- Remind yourself that saying "no" to sex before marriage also involves saying "no" to emotional attachment and to any physical involvement (such as kissing, petting, and so on) in your friendships with guys.
- Decide in advance what is off limits emotionally and physically.
- Your motto should be clearly communicated to guys: *Until I say, "I do" in marriage, I don't!*

4. **Cautiously guard your conversations with guys.**

Deep, lengthy conversations (sharing personal feelings or personal problems with each other) can deepen a young man's affection for you (and yours for him), leading the two of you to want a closer relationship than friendship. Try to limit your conversations in both how often and how long you talk. Keep your conversations as light and fun as possible.

5. **Stand on guard when you hear sweet talk.**

Girls are easily swayed by sweet words. Don't let these phrases cause you to violate your standards. Here are three examples of "sweet talk" (or lines guys might use to get girls to give in) and some possible responses you could give to stand your ground:

a. He might say: "But everybody's doing it."
   You might say: "Maybe, but I'm not everybody."

b. He might say: "Why not, are you scared?"
   You might say: "Yes, I'm scared of venereal disease, AIDS, pregnancy, and all of the other negative consequences of premarital sex."

c. He might say: "If you really loved me, you would say yes."
   You might say: "If you really loved me, you wouldn't ask."

let's talk about it

1. Have you set standards for yourself in regard to your friendships with guys? If so, what are they? If not, what would you say are some good standards that you can adopt and commit to live by?

2. How often and how much time do you spend talking on the telephone (or e-mail and computer messaging) with guys? Would you say that your conversations are moving you toward building friendships or romance?

3. Is there a need for you to make any changes in your relationships with guys to focus more on building friendships that would please God? If so, what changes should you make and when will you make those changes?

let's pray about it

Talk to God about the whole issue of purity, as it relates to your personal situation. If you have allowed negative influences to affect your purity in the past, confess it to God and recommit your purity to Him. Ask Him to help you keep your promise to abstain from sex until marriage and to honor Him with your body, mind, spirit, and soul.

If we confess our sins, He is faithful and righteous to forgive us our sins and to cleanse us from all unrighteousness.

1 John 1:9

Note: If you have allowed your relationships with guys to progress too far emotionally or physically, don't give up. Read the section at the end of this session called "Is it too late for me?" You can turn your life around and start fresh today in this area of purity.

My Heart Belongs to Him — My Identity

Here's what I discovered in this session:

POINT OF DISCOVERY

Here your daughter will record the key principles that she has learned in this session (those truths that stood out to her the most). If your daughter needs help, feel free to offer suggestions.

Because my heart belongs to Him, I will:

PERSONAL ACTION STEPS

Your daughter will record the personal changes she plans to make in her life as a result of what she has learned. Again, feel free to offer suggestions if she needs help.

NOTE: Have your daughter select one or two action points that she most wants to apply, and then have her write it (them) on the Personal Action Steps sheet on page 3 of her book.

keep moving

This section features additional projects. They are designed to help your daughter deepen her experience, and to encourage you to participate in her growth process. Feel free to use one or more of the assignments or projects presented, or use your creativity to create one or two of your own.

Try one or more of the following options this week:

A. Write a letter to God. Tell Him about those things in your life that you need to avoid or change to better guard your purity. Ask Him to cleanse you from all unrighteousness and to help you guard your purity morally, emotionally, and physically. Then talk to Him about your future husband. Pray that if it is His will for you to get married, that He would walk with your future husband day by day and that He would protect his purity and guard his heart. (You may want to keep this letter in your Bible or somewhere special, so that you can pull it out and read it to God in prayer from time to time.)

B. Write a letter to your future husband. Tell him how you are committed to guarding your purity morally, emotionally, and physically with God's help. Express to him that you want to present yourself to him as the special gift God desires you to be for him. Tell him about your prayers for your future marriage relationship and life together, as well as your prayers for him and his protection as a man of God. (If and when you marry, you can share this letter with your husband on your wedding night!)

C. You may want to keep a special journal with letters to your future husband. In your journal you can occasionally write about your hopes and dreams for your future life together. This is a great way to express your feelings of romantic love in a wholesome and healthy way. This would also make a great wedding gift!

Is It Too Late For Me?

Some of you may be thinking, *Is it too late for me? I've already given away my priceless gift.* If you opened your gift too soon, don't be discouraged. God is the author of new beginnings. Bring your broken heart before Him and ask Him to forgive you of your sins (see 1 John 1:9). Now is the time to confess your sins to God and seek His forgiveness.

Then, recommit yourself to a higher standard. Claim God's promise that He will forgive and make you clean again. Once you have done that, leave that sin there with Him. Repent, or turn away from your sin, and walk in newness of life. God has wiped your slate clean! Isaiah 1:18 says, "Come now, and let us reason together," says the Lord, "Though your sins are as scarlet, they will be as white as snow; though they are red like crimson, they will be like wool."

The next step is for you to change your lifestyle (morally, emotionally, and physically), and guard yourself against engaging in the same behaviors of your past. Make a new commitment to God to abstain from sex from this point until marriage (see Philippians 3:13).

Remember, moral purity helps you guard your emotional purity, which helps to guard your physical purity. You can develop moral purity and emotional purity by first renewing your mind. Romans 12:2a says, "And do not be conformed to this world, but be transformed by the renewing of your mind." You can do this by spending more time with God in prayer, getting into a good Bible study, spending time with other Christians, and so on. Trust God to help you keep your commitment by giving Him control of your life. Acknowledge Him in all of your day-to-day choices, including entertainment choices, and choices of friends (see Proverbs 3:5,6).

Although you might be experiencing some consequences of your sin, don't live in condemnation of your past (see Romans 8:1). Once you've confessed your sin with a sincere heart before the Lord, He has forgiven you and remembers your sin against you no more (see Hebrews 8:12 and Jeremiah 31:34). You are not damaged goods. You are a beloved child of God if you have believed in Him and received Him as Lord of your life. Don't let Satan deceive you or defeat you. Accept God's forgiveness, claim His promises, and experience His peace, freedom, and joy!

There is therefore now no condemnation for those who are in Christ Jesus. For the law of the spirit of life in Christ Jesus has set you free from the law of sin and death.

Romans 8:1-2

Important Note:

Mom, it's time to start working out the details of your daughter's Celebration Ceremony. Refer to chapter 3 at the beginning of this book for instructions and helps.

Making Wise Entertainment Choices

... Examine everything carefully;
hold fast to that which is good;
abstain from every form of evil.
1 Thessalonians 5:21-22

Reflection

To review the previous session and to follow up on projects and assignments, ask your daughter the following four questions:

1. Thinking back over the previous session, what life-changing truth would you say stood out most to you?

2. How are you doing on your "Personal Action Steps" from the last session?

3. What progress have you made with your "Keep Moving" assignments and/or projects from the previous session? (Be sure to encourage her to complete those assignments or projects that she has not yet completed.)

4. Is there anything else from the previous session that you would like to talk about?

Focus

You are what you consume. Just as what you feed your body determines your physical health, what you feed your mind will determine your spiritual, mental, and emotional health.

OBJECTIVES:

You will help your daughter learn how to make wise entertainment choices as you guide her to:

- Consider the influence of entertainment choices on her life.

- Examine the dangers of spending too much time on media entertainment.

- Understand her parents' right and responsibility to guide her entertainment choices.

- Learn how to evaluate entertainment choices.

- Evaluate her current entertainment diet and existing personal videos, CDs, and tapes to determine what changes may be necessary for a healthier entertainment diet.

This section features a
fictional story and related
discussion questions. It
introduces your daughter to
the topic and sparks an
interest in the material to be
covered in this session.
Read the story aloud
together, then discuss the
questions.

THE GARBAGE DUMP

After having lunch out with their dad, Haley and Kaitlyn walked past an alley on the way to the car. The girls noticed a horrible smell and immediately began fanning their noses. "What's that smell?" asked Kaitlyn.

"Oh, it's just the garbage dump in the alley," replied Dad laughingly. "A few more steps and you won't be able to smell it any more."

"I hope not!" exclaimed Kaitlyn. "It really smells awful!"

During the ride home, Kaitlyn asked Haley (who was reading a book) to scan the radio for a good station. "There, stop there!" shouted Kaitlyn. "I love that song!"

Right away Dad noticed that the words to the song were not good for the girls and him to be listening to. He quickly reached down and turned to a station he often listens to, prompting immediate objections. "Dad! Why'd you do that? That's one of our favorite songs!" Kaitlyn protested. Then glancing at Kaitlyn through his rear view mirror he asked, "Do you know what that song is about?"

"Oh, I don't really listen to the words, Dad," replied Kaitlyn. "I just like the beat."

"But you have to look beyond the beat and understand what the words are saying," he said in a serious tone. "That song is talking about sex outside of marriage, as if it's okay! It's totally inappropriate for you. In fact, that song's message is teaching you the direct opposite of what your mom and I have taught you about sex, Katie." Then pausing momentarily he said, "I want you to understand that the words to these songs get into your mind and spirit and can influence you to make bad choices. There's an old saying that goes, 'Garbage in, garbage out.'"

"I've heard this speech before," said Haley, looking up from her book.

"Remember that garbage dump we passed earlier?" asked Dad.

"How could I forget?" said Kaitlyn.

"How would you like me to bring some of that garbage home and dump it into your room?"

"Gross!" exclaimed both girls fanning their noses and laughing.

"Well, I was just wondering," he said, "If you wouldn't want garbage dumped into your room, why would you allow it to be dumped into your mind?" Then turning around to meet Kaitlyn face to face, as he stopped at a light, he said, "Everything, whether good or bad, that goes into your mind will affect your thoughts, words, attitudes, actions, and values. How do you think your life might eventually smell if you keep listening to that garbage?"

With a puzzled look on her face, Kaitlyn asked, "So you think that all of our music is garbage, Dad?"

"No, all of it isn't garbage. You have to take the time to evaluate each song to find out what message the singer is trying to get across. Like the Bible says, ' … Examine everything carefully; hold fast to that which is good; abstain from every form of evil.' Now, that doesn't apply to only music, but also to television, movies, videos, magazines, and any other form of entertainment or teaching. Keep the good and throw away the garbage. That way you can avoid developing an unpleasant odor in your life."

"Okay, Dad," said Kaitlyn, "I get your point. But do we have to listen to this oldies music?" Everyone laughed.

let's talk about it

1. Do you think most kids would say that they really don't listen to the words of a song? Do you believe that is true? Why or why not?

2. Do you think the words to songs matter? Why or why not?

3. Do you avoid songs, movies, television programs, and magazines with immoral messages about sex, violence, bad language, and drugs? Why or why not?

> *… Examine everything carefully; hold fast to that which is good; abstain from every form of evil.*
> 1 Thessalonians 5:21-22

get real

Would you be willing to dump garbage into your room? Of course not! But every day, millions of young people and adults are dumping garbage into their minds by making poor entertainment choices. Much of today's entertainment—like TV, movies, music, and magazines—teaches wrong attitudes and sends negative messages about sex, drugs, violence, greed, selfishness, and other areas of life. These messages can be very damaging because they can influence the way you think, act, and relate to others.

In fact, media entertainment is so powerful in our society that it actually influences what clothes we wear, what shoes we wear, what cars we drive, and what we believe is "hot" and what's "not."

In addition to being influenced, if you spend too much time entertaining yourself with media, important areas of your life might suffer, like your grades and your relationships with family and friends. You probably won't be motivated to use and improve your God-given talents such as drawing, painting, playing an instrument, playing a sport, and so on. All you'll care about is finding something to entertain yourself with. In fact, you may even forget how to have fun without media entertainment.

This section gives an overview of the topic. It gives your daughter "the big picture" as it is in our world today; for example "this is what's happening out there—this is what young women are facing." It will help your daughter relate to the topic on a personal level.

Tip:

You might want to cite current news events (clip a news or magazine article or two if you can). Look for articles on topics such as violence on school campuses, the way kids dress today, or the way they view sex and guy/girl relationships, as possible evidence of the influence of media entertainment.

let's talk about it

1. Write down some of the things you have purchased or received as gifts because you saw them on a television commercial, movie, or billboard, or in a magazine (clothing, shoes, video games, or other stuff):

My Heart Belongs to Him — My Identity

2. How often have you and your friends gotten together and had fun without a television, videotape, video game, the Internet, or a CD player to entertain you?

3. What are some ways that you can have fun without those things?

    Here are some suggestions: group games (non-electronic) such as "Charades," board games, bowling, miniature golf, skating, Christian concerts, mountain climbing, nature walks, fishing, canoeing, water parks, service projects, youth group involvement, and so on.

4. On an average, how much time are you spending in a day ...

    watching television? _____

    watching movies or videos? _____

    listening to music? _____

    surfing the Internet? _____

    playing computer or video games? _____

    reading books? _____

    communicating with friends through e-mail or a chat room? _____

    reading magazines? _____

Tip:
Your child may not realize how much time she spends doing these things, so take a few minutes to talk about what she did the last two or three days and make some time estimates.

5. Do you think you're spending too much time entertaining yourself?

6. What would you say are some of the dangers of spending too much time on entertainment?

Suggested answers: You can share the following dangers.

- You can suffer real consequences as a result of imitating what you learn from media. Though television, movies, and music may not always show the consequences of premarital sex, if you imitate what you see or hear, you will have some real consequences to suffer for your bad choices. You could get a sexually transmitted disease. Or you might become pregnant, and then go through the struggles of having and raising a child—which may include forgoing your education and future career plans. Your reputation is tarnished and you may have a lot of trouble getting a nice guy to pay attention to you. Or you carry guilt and anxiety into your future marriage, affecting your sexual intimacy and relationship with your husband. And the list goes on. Real choices have real consequences.

- You can waste a lot of time. Often the time teenagers spend entertaining themselves far outweighs the time they spend educating themselves.

- You can stifle your creativity. If you are being constantly entertained, you probably will not be motivated to use and improve your God-given talents. You probably won't be motivated to go after things that require effort and imagination.

- You can become lazy and inactive. It's very easy for kids—and adults—to become very passive, spending their time caring only about being entertained.

THE INFLUENCE OF TELEVISION AND MOVIES

The average teenager (ages 12 to 17) watches approximately 23 hours of television each week! There's no question that television can influence you. Like you learned in the story, "garbage in, garbage out." In other words, whatever you put into your mind is how you will live your life. You live what you learn.

Unfortunately, TV programs and movies are not usually made with Christian values as guidelines, so you rarely see the right values being shown. For instance, you rarely see sex and romance between a husband and wife. Instead you see sexual intimacy being shared between people who are dating, living together before marriage, or having an "affair" (committing adultery). There are also a lot of television and movie scenes where you see people resorting to violence to settle disagreements, using drugs and alcohol to cope with the pressures of life, hurting people to get what they want, and more.

My Heart Belongs to Him — My Identity

1. What is your favorite television program? What is it teaching you about life? Relationships? How to handle conflicts or problems?

2. What is your favorite movie? What does it teach you about life? Relationships? How to handle conflicts or problems?

    Here's an example of how to evaluate something using these three questions:

    Movie: "The Sound of Music"

    What does it teach me about life?

    *   Life is full of ups and downs. Looking on the bright side of things helps you enjoy each day rather than just survive each day.

    *   Money doesn't buy happiness. Happiness is cultivated in the heart.

    What does it teach me about relationships?

    *   People are meant to be valued.

    *   There is strength in pulling together as a family during a crisis.

    What does it teach about how to handle conflict and problems?

    *   Communication is the key to conflict resolution.

3. How might these programs affect you now and in the future?

4. If movies and television programs were made with Christian values as guidelines, what values, messages and scenes would you see? Can you think of any movies or TV programs where these values are shown?

Here are a few examples of Christian values they might see:

- Intimacy and romance portrayed between a husband and wife

- Commitment in marriage, even through tough times

- Commitment and loyalty in friendships

- People drawing from God and from family and friends to help cope with pressures in life

- People treating other people the way they want to be treated

- Teenagers encouraging their peers to make right choices, including saving sex and romance for marriage and having respect for parents, teachers, and other adults

5. Do you think that people sometimes imitate what they see on TV and in the movies? How can you tell?

Tip:
You might want to mention the current condition of our society— today's crime rate, high rate of teen pregnancy, outbreak of violence on school campuses, high rate of drug and alcohol use among teens, high rate of divorce, and so on as evidence that people do imitate what they see on TV and in the movies, as well as what they hear in the lyrics of today's music.

THE POWER AND INFLUENCE OF MUSIC

Music is often used to influence your thoughts, feelings, and actions. In movies, music is used to set the mood and hold your attention. On television, it is used in commercials to sell products. Why? Because the product owners know that the "jingle" or song from the commercial will help you remember their product when you go shopping or when you need or want something. They know the power that music has to influence people.

Some songs and music videos seem so romantic. But often they don't teach biblical values. In them you see or hear about a guy and girl, who are not married, in each other's arms, eating by candlelight, taking showers together, and sleeping together. The message is that anything that makes you feel good is the right thing to do. The consequences of such behavior are never mentioned. Everyone in the song or the video seems to be so happy and so in love. It all seems so good … so right. And girls who are listening or watching think to themselves, "Oh, how romantic. I want that." Then for many of them fantasy leads to reality, and they end up giving in to the strong desires to imitate what they heard in the song or saw in the music video.

Another example is love songs that promote dependency on another person, with lyrics like … "I can't live, if living is without you …" or "Please understand, if love ends, then I promise you, I promise you that I shall never breathe again …" The problem with these songs is that they encourage you to put all of your faith and trust in another person, when God is the only One who can truly meet all of your needs.

Tip:
You might want to ask your daughter, "Have you ever known a girl who thought she was so in love with a guy that she believed she couldn't live without him? And then, when he dumped her, she actually felt like she was going to die? What about you? Have you ever felt this way?"

let's talk about it

1. Can you think of any songs or music videos that portray premarital sex as if it's okay? How do those songs make you feel?

2. Can you think of any songs that promote dependency on another person? How do these songs make you feel?

3. Have you ever listened to songs that made you feel blue or down on yourself? What were you going through that caused you to listen to those kinds of songs? Did the song make you feel better or worse?

4. List three of your favorite songs. What is the main message in each song?

Tip:

Here is an example that you can share of how dangerous communicating on-line can be if you're not careful:

A 12-year-old girl who may have an online relationship with someone she thinks is her age, may actually be communicating with a 40-year-old man who has bad intentions. There have actually been real-life cases where an adult pretending to be a young person developed an on-line relationship with a teenager, gained her trust, then enticed her into giving private information that led to her home or school, putting her and her family in great danger.

WHAT ABOUT THE INTERNET?

You can find all sorts of games, Web sites, chat rooms, photos, music, and more on the Internet. Unfortunately, not everything available to you on the Internet is good. When you are "surfing the net" you have access to all kinds of information, including material with violent or sexually inappropriate content, such as pornography (material like films, pictures, books, or songs) that is meant to cause sexual excitement. As with other forms of entertainment, you have to be wise and make right choices.

Communicating on-line can also be dangerous if you're not careful. For example, when you're in a chat room or sending e-mail back and forth, you don't know anything about the real person you are communicating with. They may not be the age, sex, or type of person they are portraying themselves to be. Be careful to use extreme caution while surfing the net, and avoid chat rooms and Web sites that you know are not appropriate for you.

let's talk about it

1. What do you usually do on the Internet? Do you feel you are making appropriate choices?

Tip:
Here are some additional questions you may want to ask, if your daughter spends time on the Internet:

- What type of chat rooms have you visited?
- Have you found the conversations in those chat rooms to be appropriate?
- Why or why not?
- What type of Web sites have you visited?
- Have you developed any on-line relationships?
- Are your conversations appropriate?
- If not, what can you do about this?

2. Can you think of some ways that you can help yourself avoid bad content on the Internet?

   Suggested answer: Ask your parents to either sign up with a filtered Internet service provider or purchase filtering software such as "Cybersitter®" or "Net Nanny®." You should ask friends not to send you any negative or damaging material.

let's pray about it

Talk to God about your choices of television programs, movies, music, and so on. Ask Him to give you the wisdom and the courage to be wise as you make entertainment choices every day, so that your choices would honor Him and help you grow in healthy, wholesome ways.

STOP HERE! If you prefer to do this session in two parts, you may find this to be a natural place to stop. However, if you want to complete this session in one sitting, please continue.

get direction

Have you ever eaten sunflower seeds? The first thing you do before you eat one is to crack the shell to see whether the seed inside is good or if it's rotten. What do you do when you crack the shell and find a rotten seed inside? Do you eat it? No way! You toss it. It should be the same with your choices of entertainment. Find out what the message is, and if it's rotten, toss it! Have the wisdom and the courage to change the channel, turn the station, go to a different Web site or chat room, or close the book or magazine! Just as you would not feed your body rotten food, refuse to feed your spirit rotten food. Both the body and the spirit need the proper nourishment to survive and grow.

let's talk about it

1. Most of the songs Mary listens to are love songs, including the music videos she watches. The songs send the message that it's romantic for boyfriends and girlfriends to believe that they belong to each other, and that premarital sex is okay, normal, and good. Most of the music videos show young men and women involved in romantic relationships that include passionate hugging, kissing, and sex. Everyone seems to be happy and in love. How can Mary's choice of entertainment affect her?

   Suggested answer: She can be enticed by the idea of romance portrayed and want to experience it in her own life. She may also be taken in by the fantasy of it all and not think about the consequences until she is experiencing them (lost virginity, unwanted pregnancy, sexually transmitted disease, a broken heart, and so on).

2. Rebecca's favorite television program about a group of teens shows kids being disrespectful to parents, teachers, and other adults. They skip classes, are involved sexually, experiment with drugs and alcohol, and use profanity. How can Rebecca's choice of entertainment affect her?

   Suggested answer: She can begin to think that this type of behavior is "cool." She could begin to imitate these behaviors, especially if she sees them bringing positive results (like popularity with other kids) in her eyes. She may ruin her reputation in the process and suffer negative consequences as a result of bad choices.

My Heart Belongs to Him — My Identity

3. Jenny's favorite radio station plays Christian music. All of the songs send positive messages about what life is like when you trust Jesus Christ as your Savior and Lord. The songs have messages of peace, hope, and love, and they encourage people to make wise choices. How can Jenny's choice of entertainment affect her?

Suggested answer: She is allowing herself to be influenced by the truth and will be influenced to make wise choices. She is building a hedge of protection around herself by filling her mind with positive messages. Her character will be strengthened, and she can become a positive influence in the lives of others.

LET GOD'S WORD BE YOUR GUIDE

Because your heart belongs to God, He wants to be the number one influence in your life. Proverbs 3:5-6 says, "Trust in the Lord with all your heart and do not lean on your own understanding. In all your ways acknowledge Him, and He will make your paths straight." Are you acknowledging Him in your entertainment choices so that He can guide you? Or are you getting lost in the whirlwind of evil messages swirling around much of today's entertainment? If so, you can make a change today. You can start acknowledging God from this day forward in all of your entertainment choices, so that you will make the right ones.

let's talk about it

Look up each of the following passages. How can these truths help us make good choices about the media?

1. Psalm 101:2,3

Suggested answer: We are to refuse to watch or read things that teach bad morals or that compromise our standards. When we give in to the temptation to watch or read those things, we allow ourselves to be influenced by their negative messages.

2. 2 Timothy 2:16

Suggested answer: Not only is this an admonishment not to gossip, lie, or bear false witness, it can also apply to listening to worldly and empty chatter, which can often be found in the lyrics of today's songs. The warning is that this kind of talk (or lyrics) can lead to further ungodliness (unwise life choices).

3. **2 Timothy 2:22**

Suggested answer: "To flee" means don't just walk away, but run away quickly! A lot of today's media entertainment glorifies youthful lusts, such as sexual immorality, drug and alcohol use, wild parties, and so on. This Bible verse tells us to run from those things (avoid TV programs, movies, music, magazines, and other media that portray these things as a normal part of life), and it also tells us to pursue or go after righteousness. A righteous life doesn't just happen. We have to make right choices in life and grow in our relationship with God; this will result in a righteous life.

4. **2 Corinthians 5:9**

Suggested answer: According to this Scripture, our ambition in life should be to please God in everything we do. This includes our entertainment choices. Before we watch a TV program or a movie, or listen to the radio or a CD, and before we read a magazine or visit a Web site on the Internet, we should first ask ourselves, "Will this please God?" If we cannot answer *yes*, we should make a better choice.

SUBMIT TO YOUR PARENTS' AUTHORITY

God has given your parents the responsibility of guiding you into adulthood. Even though your heart belongs to God and you are responsible to Him for your actions, your parents are also responsible for guarding your heart until you are an adult. God expects your parents to help you develop godly character and good values. It is their responsibility to decide what you should be allowed to watch (on TV, videotapes, and in the movies), what music you should be allowed to listen to, and what books or magazines you're allowed to read.

Because God holds your parents accountable for guiding you properly, they must hold you accountable for making wise choices. And since they must, as you will, give an account to God for your actions, you should obey them and listen to their wise advice. Keep in mind that they have your best interests at heart, and that they are simply obeying God in working to help you develop into a godly, courageous woman.

let's talk about it

1. Read Hebrews 13:17. What does this Bible verse say about your parents (or anyone else) in authority over you?

Suggested answer: It says that you should obey them and submit to them because they have been put in your life by God to watch over your soul. Your submission and obedience will profit your life. Note, however, that obedience to authorities and parents must never violate God's Word. Peter reminds us in Acts 5:29b, "We must obey God rather than men."

2. QUESTIONS TO ASK MOM:

- What kind of music did you listen to when you were my age?

- What kinds of movies and magazines did you like?

- In what ways did your entertainment choices influence you?

- Can you determine how your entertainment choices as a teenager may be affecting your life today?

- How did your parents feel about your entertainment choices when you were my age?

get going

Is your entertainment diet healthy? How can your current entertainment diet affect your life both now and in the future? Do you need to make some changes to your entertainment diet? If so, how and when do you plan to make those changes? Here are some ways that you can evaluate media before you watch, listen, or read:

The "Phil. 4:8" test:

... whatever is true, whatever is honorable, whatever is right, whatever is pure, whatever is lovely, whatever is of good repute, if there is any excellence and if anything worthy of praise, dwell on these things.

Philippians 4:8

1. **Ask yourself whether it meets the "Phil. 4:8" test.** God knows how our minds work, so He has given us some very clear guidelines in Philippians 4:8 for what we should and should not be exposing ourselves to. If we dwell on those things that meet the "Phil. 4:8" test, then we will gain incredible benefits in our minds and lives.

2. **Ask your parents to preview it first.** Or have them learn about the content of a movie before deciding if you can see it. Note: Don't depend on movie ratings as a guide. Look on the Internet for sites that tell you what's actually in a movie to help you determine whether it is appropriate and worthy of you seeing it. (There is a list of suggested Web sites in the *Mother's Guide*.)

3. **Ask for a recommendation from a trustworthy friend.** Here are four questions to help you determine whether or not it is suitable for you:

   - What will it teach me (what is the message)?

   - Does the right or good win over the bad (for TV, movies, and videos)?

   - Are real consequences to sin exposed?

   - Where does it stand in regard to relationships, sex, violence, language, and sorcery?

4. **Check the back of music tapes or CDs for a rating or ask if copies of the lyrics are available for review.** Sometimes you can preview music in the store before purchasing it by either reading the lyrics from the CD insert, or by listening to the lyrics on headphones.

5. **Since it is our aim to please Him in everything we do, ask yourself two simple questions, according to your research, before making an entertainment choice.**

For as he [a person] thinks within himself, so he is.
Proverbs 23:7a

- Would Jesus want to watch this ... listen to this ... read this?

- Would this program/video/movie/song/book/magazine please Him?

If you can answer no to either question, you know you need to make a different choice ... a better choice.

A word about movie and music ratings:

So often you hear people say, "I would never watch a PG-13, or an R-rated movie, but there's nothing wrong with G or PG movies." Believe it or not, there are some G and PG rated movies that have very negative messages, and some include messages that are contrary to God's Word. Many are packed with sex or sexual suggestions that are totally inappropriate for Christians. Therefore G and PG rated movies are not always good or appropriate just because of their ratings. Remember that even these movies are not typically made with Christian values in mind. Occasionally, you may approve a movie that has some amount of inappropriate content because you may feel that your daughter will benefit from the overall message of the movie. This is totally up to your discretion. Encourage your daughter to evaluate all movies, including those rated G and PG, rather than let the world decide what is good or not good for her to watch.

The following sources offer helpful information regarding the evaluation of music, movies, and videos:

- www.crosswalk.com
- www.screenit.com
- www.movieguide.org or 1-800-899-6684
- *Plugged In* (A magazine published by Focus on the Family, 1-800-A-Family)
- *Preview* (A magazine published by Family Movie and TV Review, 1-800-807-8071)

The main thing to remember is that because your heart belongs to God, you want to make sure that you are feeding your mind and spirit those things that will help you to draw closer to Him and grow in Christian character. A great result of your strong relationship with God and strength of character is that you will have a positive influence in the lives of others. What you don't want to do is train your mind and soul to be lazy, to waste time, to be greedy, to be violent, or to be sexually immoral! All entertainment is not bad, but a lot of it is. Although your mind works like a computer according to the "garbage in, garbage out" rule, the exciting thing is that you are not a computer. You have the power to choose what goes in your mind and what you will dwell on.

 ## let's pray about it

Talk to God about what you learned in this session and ask Him to give you the wisdom, strength, and courage to change your entertainment diet where necessary. Request that He help you with creative ways and opportunities in challenging your friends to consider their entertainment diet.

Here's what I discovered in this session:

POINT OF DISCOVERY

Here your daughter will record the key principles that she has learned in this session (those truths that stood out to her the most). If your daughter needs help, feel free to offer suggestions.

Because my heart belongs to Him, I will:

PERSONAL ACTION STEPS

Your daughter will record the personal changes she plans to make in her life as a result of what she has learned. Again, feel free to offer suggestions if she needs help.

NOTE: Have your daughter select one or two action points that she most wants to apply, and then have her write it (them) on the Personal Action Steps sheet on page 3 of her book.

keep moving

This section features additional projects. They are designed to help your daughter deepen her experience, and to encourage you to participate in her growth process. Feel free to use one or more of the assignments or projects presented, or use your creativity to create one or two of your own.

Try these fun activities during the next week:

A. Rent the Disney movie "The Little Mermaid" to watch with your mom or dad. Measure the movie against God's Word and then decide together whether or not it was a good choice. What was good about it? What was questionable or wrong about it?

Suggested answer: Even a movie like "The Little Mermaid" can contain some questionable sections if you watch with a discerning eye. For example: Ariel was unhappy with her life as it was, and therefore became disobedient to her father and rebellious.

- She wouldn't listen to reason or counsel from those who loved her.

- She went to see a witch who she thought could help her become a human.

- She put her father in great danger as she tried to accomplish her own will and desires.

- Ariel's father exchanged his life for hers by selling his soul to the witch.

- Ariel sacrificed everything she stood for as well as her relationships with her family and friends to get what she wanted.

- With graphic violence, the film shows Ursula, the witch, being killed by the prince, which set all the other mermaids free, including Ariel's father.

- The movie ended with Ariel's father looking longingly at Ariel and Prince Eric, making this statement, "She really did love him. Children have to be free to lead their own lives." And with the magic of his sword, he turned Ariel into a human being. His parting words condoned all of her wrong attitudes and actions for the sake of love.

$\mathcal{B}$. Clean house! Remember the "Phil. 4:8" test from Philippians? "… whatever is true, whatever is honorable, whatever is right, whatever is pure, whatever is lovely, whatever is of good repute, if there is any excellence and if anything worthy of praise, dwell on these things." Can you say that about the music you are listening to? Or the movies you watch?

Go through your home videos, CDs, and tapes with your parents and evaluate together what is good to keep and what should be tossed. (Use the questions we listed earlier in the "Get Direction" section.)

Session 8

Managing My Time Wisely

*Teach us to number our days and
recognize how few they are;
help us to spend them as we should.*
Psalm 90:12 (TLB)

Reflection

To review the previous session and to follow up on projects and assignments, ask your daughter the following four questions:

1. Thinking back over the previous session, what life-changing truth would you say stood out most to you?

2. How are you doing on your "Personal Action Steps" from the last session?

3. What progress have you made with your "Keep Moving" assignments and/or projects from the previous session? (Be sure to encourage her to complete those assignments or projects that she has not yet completed.)

4. Is there anything else from the previous session that you would like to talk about?

Focus

Your time is a treasured gift from God, and you are only given so much of it here on earth before it will eventually run out. Because your heart belongs to Him, you want to be sure you are making the most of the time you have by doing the right things for the right reasons.

OBJECTIVES:

You will help your daughter understand the importance of managing her time wisely as you guide her to:

- Examine what causes life to be so busy and discover ways to avoid the busyness trap.

- Evaluate her life to determine whether or not she is over-committed with activities and responsibilities.

- Recognize the signs, symptoms, and consequences of laziness and procrastination.

- Examine how Jesus managed His life and learn how to pattern her life after His.

- Determine her personal limits and learn how to live within them.

- Discover how to live a life of purpose by determining her life's mission and her personal gifts, talents, abilities, and priorities.

get ready

This section features a fictional story and related discussion questions. It introduces your daughter to the topic and sparks an interest in the material to be covered in this session. Read the story aloud together, then discuss the questions.

THE JUGGLING ACT

"Mom! Katie!" Haley yelled excitedly as she came charging through the front door. "I made it! I made it!"

"You made the dance team?" asked Kaitlyn as she peered out of the kitchen door.

"Yes! Can you believe it?"

"I sure can," said Mom as she embraced Haley. "I knew you could do it! I didn't have one doubt! Congratulations!" Then the three of them began screaming and jumping up and down right in the middle of the kitchen floor.

"Hey, what's all the racket about?" asked Haley's father as he walked in the front door from work. After sharing the good news, the four of them enjoyed dinner and then went out for a celebration dessert. While at the ice cream shop, Haley began telling her family about all of the things she wanted to be involved in this year in addition to the dance team. Finally, her dad interrupted saying, "Honey, I think it's great that you want to be involved in so many things. But with choir, youth group, Sunday school, clarinet lessons, keeping up with your studies, household chores, and now dance team, I think you might already be too busy."

"But Dad," protested Haley, "I just wanted to join a couple of clubs, and maybe play volleyball and run track. That's not too much. I can do it!"

"I remember when I was about your age, Haley," her mom said. "I thought I could do it all, too. I was actively involved in my church, just like you. I was also student body president at school, captain of the cheerleading squad, and I played volleyball. Not to mention my responsibilities at home, you know ... helping out around the house."

"I'll bet everyone respected you," said Haley. "And I'll bet you were popular at school and made your parents proud of you."

"Yes, at first," replied her mother. "But after awhile all of the responsibility began to wear me down. Everyone had high expectations of me. Eventually my grades began to suffer, I began having awful headaches, and it seemed as if I never had time for myself. And because I was spreading myself so thin, I wasn't doing anything as well as I knew I could.

"One day, on the way home from cheerleading practice, I began to think about the meeting that I still had to attend later that evening, and all of the

152   My Heart Belongs to Him — My Identity

homework I had to do, and the test I had to study for, and the dishes I had to wash, and … well you get the picture. Anyway, I was so exhausted. I didn't think I could do another thing."

"What happened?" asked Kaitlyn with curiosity, as Haley anxiously awaited the rest of the story.

"Well at that moment, it felt like everything was caving in on me, and I just fell apart. I broke down right there in the car. I cried and cried, for what felt like forever. My mother pulled the car over and after comforting me, we had a long heart-to-heart talk. It became very clear that I needed to back away from some things. I was doing way too much. I was completely stressed out!" she said with emphasis. "Everyone has their limits, and I had gone beyond mine."

"I wouldn't let that happen to me," said Haley. "Honest!" she pleaded.

"But it can happen to you, honey," her dad warned, "and it will … if you exceed your limits."

let's talk about it

1. Do you think Haley wanted to take on too many responsibilities? Why? Why not?

2. Do you think her parents were able to convince her that she was taking on too much? If not, what lesson might Haley have to learn the hard way?

3. Have you ever felt stressed out or like you had too many responsibilities? Share your experience.

get real

This section gives an overview of the topic. It gives your daughter "the big picture" as it is in our world today; for example "this is what's happening out there—this is what young women are facing." It will help your daughter relate to the topic on a personal level.

Life is so fast-paced today. There are microwaves to cook your food in a snap, e-mail and fax machines to send information across the world at unimaginable speeds, computers to help you think and work faster, pagers and mobile phones to provide a way to communicate on the go, and our technology just keeps increasing the pace. People of all ages are finding themselves involved in so many activities that they feel like they're performing a juggling act just to keep up with it all.

When you take on too many commitments and responsibilities, you can feel overwhelmed and stressed out. You feel the demands of everyone's expectations pulling you in all different directions, and you only have so much of yourself to give. Oftentimes, God gets crowded out altogether as you may find that you are too busy or too tired to pray, read the Bible, have regular devotions, or attend church services. When life becomes too busy, the things that really matter will suffer. Busyness will eventually catch up with you and begin to wear you out.

let's talk about it

1. Are you too busy? Check any of the following statements that are true of you.

- ◯ I can't relax.
- ◯ I don't enjoy quiet.
- ◯ I feel stressed.
- ◯ I am disorganized (messy room, locker, desk, notebook).
- ◯ I'm forgetful (books and assignments, messages for family members, events).
- ◯ I don't feel good about myself.
- ◯ I spend too much time doing things that don't really count.
- ◯ I worry about things I cannot change.
- ◯ My relationships are suffering.
- ◯ My grades are suffering.

2. Did you know that every week you are given 168 hours of time to work with? Out of these hours, 103 are managed for you. For example: You sleep an average of 56 hours per week, attend school for 40 hours per week, and spend approximately seven hours per week eating meals. How do you manage or spend the remaining 65 hours of your week?

Take a look at the following list of activities and write down the approximate number of hours per week that you spend doing each. Make sure the total hours add up to 65.

NUMBER OF HOURS	ACTIVITY
_____	Personal grooming (bathing, combing my hair, ironing clothes, dressing, etc.)
_____	Time alone with God (Bible study, devotions, prayer)
_____	Outreach (ministry to non-Christians such as witnessing)
_____	Participating in church and church-related activities (worship service, Sunday school, youth group)
_____	Interacting with parents (meaningful times of communicating one-on-one)
_____	Interacting with siblings
_____	Chores and responsibilities at home
_____	Serving (ministry to the body of Christ, using my gifts, talents, and abilities to serve—such as working with younger children, singing in the choir, playing an instrument for worship service, and so on)
_____	Entertainment at home (TV, computer, books and magazines, etc.)
_____	Talking on the telephone or through computer messaging
_____	Relaxing
_____	Sports
_____	Hobbies
_____	Lessons/clubs (gymnastics, piano, cheerleading, swimming, etc.)
_____	Entertainment with friends (movies, parties, hanging out together)
_____	Other:_____

65 HOURS TOTAL

3. After looking over the way you normally spend your remaining 65 hours, answer the following questions:

- Do you feel good about the way you spend your time?

- Is your schedule too full?

- How is your relationship with God?

- Are you carrying your share of responsibilities at home?

- Are you spending enough time with family?

- Do you have enough free time to do the things you really want to do?

- Do you need to make some changes to your daily life to better balance your time and relieve yourself from stress?

Tip:
You may want to share with your daughter that many people simply do not know how to say no. As a result, they end up taking on more than they can really handle. Help her understand that if she allows herself to become over-committed she will risk becoming overwhelmed and stressed out. When this happens, she may begin to feel a sense of failure, because when she spreads herself too thin or becomes too involved, it is almost impossible to do the best job she can in any one area. The best thing to do is to try to live a balanced life, striving to do the "best" things instead of the "good" things.

THE BUSYNESS TRAP

Many people are busy with activities and things that make their lives feel crowded, leaving no time or energy for the things that really matter. Like the student who spends too much time involved in extra-curricular activities or a part-time job, leaving her no time for rest or proper studying, so her grades begin to suffer. It is very important to make sure that your life is occupied with the things that count—those things that God wants you to do.

Many people are busy doing the right things, but their reasons for doing them might be all wrong. For example, some people do a lot of things just to please other people or to gain popularity. Some get involved in too many things because they're afraid they'll miss out on something, or because carrying a lot of responsibility pumps their ego and makes them feel good. Others take on a lot of responsibilities so that they can use their activities as an excuse to stay away from home, because they may not get along with their parents or siblings. And then there are those who overload with commitments because they feel that no one else can do those things better than they can.

You can even serve God or help other people for the wrong reasons. And when you do, it makes doing the right thing wrong. God knows your motives. He knows your reasons for doing everything you do. If you are serving Him and helping others just to impress people (or even God), or to gain their praise, honor, or respect, your service will not count eternally. When you don't serve with a heart of thankfulness and love, you will miss out on the blessings and rewards that only God can give. Remember that whatever you do, if you are doing it for the wrong reasons, it might be better not to do it at all.

let's talk about it

Look again at the way you are spending your 65 hours per week, and then answer the following questions:

1. Can you say that you are spending most of your time on the right things and for the right reasons? Why or Why not?

2. Is there an area of your life that may be suffering as a result of your commitments and activities? If so, what area might that be, and in what ways could you adjust your schedule to allow more time in that area of your life?

3. Are any of your activities helping you become the person you want to be in the future? If yes, list them and explain how they are helping you.

Tip:

Make your daughter aware that there are consequences to pay when she wastes time as a way of life. You can even ask her to think of some possible consequences of wasting time. To name a few: You can experience guilt because of all the things that go undone; or get stressed from disappointing others or from doing everything at the last minute; or suffer from depression as you watch life going on all around, while seemingly leaving you out. Time waits for no one. It is one gift that once you have spent it, you can never get it back—you can't even exchange it. If you are wise, however, you can have something to show for it.

THE OPPOSITE OF BUSYNESS

For many people who wonder where their time has gone, busyness is not the problem … it's laziness or procrastination (putting off doing something until a future time, especially for no good reason). Many teens spend hours upon hours doing nothing, just "vegging." Instead of offering to help around the house or doing their chores, they would rather lie around, play video games, or talk on the phone. Then there are the "couch potatoes" who live life in front of the television tube. Or the "loners" who spend hours closed up in their rooms, with a headset on their ears listening to music. Meanwhile, time keeps ticking as relationships with family and friends suffer, grades drop, and responsibilities are overlooked because of laziness.

Here is an example of how much time you can waste just watching television:

If you watched an average of three hours of television per day for five days each week, you would have spent 60 hours a month, and 720 hours per year in front of the tube. When you add up the numbers over the years, they equal thousands of hours of wasted time—six years of 24-hour days by the time you're 70 years old.

let's talk about it

1. How many times have you put off something you needed to do until later, or the next day? Or waited until the last minute to do a school project, study for a test, or do one of your chores? How did procrastinating make you feel?

2. What were some consequences that you've had to pay as a result of procrastinating? What did you learn from your experience?

3. If you are struggling with laziness or procrastination in some areas of your life, what are some things that you can do to improve in those areas?

let's pray about it

Talk to God about the way you have been managing your time. Ask Him to give you the wisdom and the strength to avoid busyness as well as laziness, procrastination, and wasting time. Then ask Him to help you manage your time more wisely and keep your motives (reasons) for what you do pure.

STOP HERE! If you prefer to do this session in two parts, you may find this to be a natural place to stop. However, if you want to complete this session in one sitting, please continue.

get direction

Time is one of God's greatest gifts to us. However, we are only given so much of it here on earth before it will eventually run out. No one knows when his or her time on earth is done. Because your heart belongs to Him, you want to make sure that you are making the most of the time you have by doing the right things, for the right reasons. If you are too busy, you are not using your time wisely. And if you are lazy and procrastinating as a habit, you are not using your time wisely. It goes both ways.

The truth is, you need to find balance in order to manage your time well. But balance doesn't come when you suddenly discover the magic formula for how much time to give to each activity in your life. A balanced life grows out of submitting every area of your life to the Lord, and allowing the Holy Spirit to direct your thinking and actions. This is what the Bible calls being "filled with the Spirit" and having "the mind of Christ." When you live a life balanced through God's power and direction, you can experience God's peace and joy. You can be happy with each day no matter what it brings. You won't feel hurried or anxious as a general rule, and you won't take life too seriously or too lightly. And when your time on earth is done, you will have no regrets about having wasted or misused your gift of time.

let's talk about it

1. What do the following Bible verses say to you about your life and how precious the gift of time is?

a. James 4:14

Suggested answer: No one knows when his or her earthly life will be over.

b. Ephesians 5:16

Suggested answer: Don't be foolish; instead be wise and make the most of your life and every opportunity you have for doing good.

2. What do the following Scriptures say about laziness and procrastination?

   a. Proverbs 15:19

   Suggested answer: People who are lazy will have trouble all through life.

   b. Hebrews 6:12

   Suggested answer: Instead of being lazy, we are to imitate those who through diligence inherit what God has promised.

3. What do the following verses say to you about the importance of doing the right things for the right reasons (making sure your motives are pure)?

   a. Proverbs 16:2

   Suggested answer: God knows your heart and therefore knows whether your motives are pure.

   b. Mark 8:36

   Suggested answer: It will do you no good to win the praises or approval of people if God is not pleased. Pleasing Him is what really matters in the end.

JESUS MANAGED HIS TIME WISELY

Jesus knew how important it was to manage time wisely. Even though He had a full life, He did not allow Himself to become too busy or stressed out, nor was He ever lazy. And Jesus always did everything for the right reasons. He didn't get involved in things to please other people or to become popular—only to please the Father. And when He was tired from His full schedule, He knew when to pull away and get some rest. He got plenty of exercise to keep His body in good physical shape. He did a lot of walking. Jesus also took time to enjoy life. He lived a balanced life that was fully controlled by God.

The Bible teaches us that as followers of Christ, we are to imitate Him. We are to follow His example in all things: the way He lived His life, the way He managed His time, the way He related to people, and so on. Ephesians 5:1 says, "Therefore be imitators of God, as beloved children."

Jesus clearly understood His purpose on earth, and He made sure that the way He spent His time lined up with that purpose. He knew His divine purpose in life was to do the will of the Father, therefore His number one priority in life was His relationship with God. According to Matthew 6:33 your relationship with God should also be your number one priority.

let's talk about it

What do the following Bible verses say about the things that should be important in your life if your relationship with God is your number one priority?

1. Colossians 4:2

   Suggested answer: Devote yourself to prayer and have an attitude of thankfulness.

2. 2 Timothy 2:15, Acts 17:11

   Suggested answer: Study the Bible eagerly and diligently.

3. Hebrews 10:25

   Suggested answer: Be sure to participate in regular fellowship with other Christians and faithful church attendance.

4. Acts 22:15

   Suggested answer: Witness to the life-changing power of the Lord and share your faith with others.

5. Psalm 100:2

   Suggested answer: Serve God with gladness and worship Him.

6. Galatians 5:13

   Suggested answer: Serve one another in love.

get going

There are so many things available today to help us manage our time. There are planners, calendars, appointment books, electronic organizers, computer software, and more. You may find one or more of those things to be helpful, or you may prefer schedules or "things to do" lists.

It's really not important what you use to manage your time. What's really important is that you manage your time wisely. Because your heart belongs to Him, you want to make sure that you are making the most of the time He has given you by keeping your priorities in order. Spend your time doing those things that you know He would want you to do. Spend time with Him. Spend time with family and friends. Study. Serve Him (through serving others) with your gifts and talents. Enjoy fun activities. Take time out for rest and relaxation.

This is the life application section of the session. It includes practical guidelines and action points to help your daughter live out what she has learned.

DETERMINE YOUR PRIORITIES

Your priorities are those things that are of most importance in your life, and those things that you give the most time and energy to. Some people might say that the order of their priorities might look like this:

1. God

2. Family

3. Ministry to others

4. Myself

5. School

Other priorities could be extra-curricular activities, a part-time job (if allowed by parents), hobbies, and so on. In order to manage your time wisely, you must first have your priorities in the right order. You must know what is important to God and to you, and make those things your priorities. But it's not enough to make God the first priority in your life. You need to give Him access and control in every area. Only as you walk in the Spirit day-by-day, and minute-by-minute, will you truly get your priorities right. Read over Galatians 5:16-26 and step out in His power.

KNOW YOUR LIMITS AND OBSERVE THEM

Know how much you can handle before taking on activities and responsibilities. Everyone has limits. When you go beyond your limits, you can push yourself too hard, too fast, or too far. And when you do, you can experience unhealthy stress, frustration, depression, a sense of failure, anger, or other potentially harmful emotions.

You need to know when to say, "Enough!" And you need to understand that it's okay to say no, even to a good thing when it doesn't line up with your priorities and goals, or when your schedule is already full. Don't allow yourself to feel guilty when you must say no. God will honor your wisdom and maturity, and people will understand after you've given a loving and gentle explanation. Staying within your limits will help keep you on track for fulfilling your life's purpose and will help keep you healthy—body, mind, and spirit.

let's talk about it

1. Write out your list of priority activities on a separate sheet of paper, and post it where you can see it regularly.

Tip:
The activity in this section will be much easier if you and your daughter work together.

2. List every optional (extracurricular) activity that you have chosen to be involved in on your sheet too.

3. For each of the activities that you listed on your sheet, answer the following questions adapted from *Parenting Today's Adolescent* [1]:

   ❦ How does this activity benefit me as a person?

   ❦ How will this affect my relationship with others in my family?

   ❦ Is anyone pressuring me to participate in this?

   ❦ Will this add too much stress to my life?

   ❦ What could suffer as a result of me participating in this activity?

   ❦ Do I feel this is something God wants me to be involved in?

4. According to your answers in question 3, are there any activities you need to release yourself from? What are some ways that you can back away from these activities with honor and integrity?

let's pray about it

Talk to God about giving you wisdom regarding how you spend your time. Ask Him to show you what areas in your life He wants you to cut back on, and what areas He wants you to spend more time on. Then ask Him to guide you as you make those changes and give you the courage to follow through. And if you feel the temptation to add extra activities that don't line up with your current priorities and goals, or the temptation to waste time through laziness and procrastination, pray and ask God to help you. Remember, He will always be there for you!

My Heart Belongs to Him — My Identity

Here's what I discovered in this session:

Here your daughter
will record the key
principles that she
has learned in this
session (those truths
that stood out to her
the most). If your
daughter needs
help, feel free to
offer suggestions.

Because my heart belongs to Him, I will:

PERSONAL
ACTION STEPS

Your daughter will
record the personal
changes she plans
to make in her life as
a result of what she
has learned. Again,
feel free to offer
suggestions if she
needs help.

NOTE: Have your
daughter select one
or two action points
that she most wants
to apply, and then
have her write it
(them) on the
Personal Action
Steps sheet on page
3 of her book.

keep moving

Listed below are four additional steps you can take to help you manage your time wisely. Work through each one carefully over the next week or two.

A. **Write out a personal mission statement that represents who you want to become and what you want to be about.**

Earlier you determined your key priorities. From these priorities, write out a personal mission statement. This statement will help you manage your time, keep your priorities in order, and reach your goals in life. Your mission statement is not written in stone. It may change as you get older. The whole purpose is to state what you are about at this time in your life.

Here's an example of a personal mission statement: "My mission is to glorify God in my life and in my relationships, and to use my unique gifts, talents, and abilities to influence others for Christ."

B. **Determine your unique gifts, talents, and abilities.**

1. Spend time in prayer, asking God to help you discover the unique gifts, talents, and abilities He has given you. List them here.

2. Consider the following questions and discuss them with your mom and dad:

- What dreams, thoughts, or ideas about your future do you have that just won't go away—ones that cause your heart to flutter when you think about them?

- Do you feel that God may be leading you in a certain direction, such as writing, speaking, law, medicine, sports, teaching, missions, ministry, etc.?

- What are you really passionate about?

- What are you really good at doing?

C. **Set goals for yourself according to your mission statement.**

1. After spending time in prayer, and answering the questions listed above carefully and prayerfully, write down one or two life goals that you feel you may want to pursue. Hint: These may be dreams of yours that just will not go away—dreams that you believe God has given you. Or perhaps, dreams that you've noticed your parents, teachers, and other leaders steering you toward.

Life Goals:

a.

b.

2. There are various types of goals: personal, family, household, spiritual, physical, educational, and so on. You might want to determine a short-term goal (to reach in the next few months) and a long-term goal (to reach during the next few years) for each. Here are some examples:

Personal: To develop a hobby I can enjoy regularly (short-term goal)

To become a godly wife and mother (long-term goal)

Family: To build a better relationship with my brothers

Household: To have my weekend chores done by 12 noon every Saturday

Spiritual: To keep a daily appointment with God before I begin my day

Physical: To exercise three times a week

Educational: To maintain at least a 3.0 GPA or B average

D. **Write out a list of action steps that will help you make your goals a reality**

List your goals (short-term and long-term). Underneath each goal, write a list of action steps. Keep in mind that this activity may take a great deal of time. You may want to do one category of goals per night or per week. You don't have to do this all at once. Also note that you will have a different number of action steps for each goal. The following is one example:

Family Goals:

Goal 1: To build a better relationship with my brothers.

Action Steps:

- Each day ask how their day went and show interest in what they have to say.

- Schedule at least one hour each week to play games with them.

- Set aside time to attend their special events (to support them)—such as football games, band competitions, or scout awards ceremonies.

- Give them a personal invitation to my special events. Tell them how much it would mean to have them there supporting me.

My Heart Belongs to Him — My Identity

Congratulations on completing this study!

Next comes your final exam.

The real test of courageous womanhood will be your journey through life.

You Can Know God Personally

God created us to have an abundant life now and for eternity. But He did not create us like robots that would automatically love and follow Him. He gave us a will and freedom to choose our eternal destination. What will you choose?

Are you 100% sure that you are going to heaven? Why do you say that?

Mark on the following scale how sure you are that you have a personal relationship with God, through Jesus Christ?

Not at all sure   1   2   3   4   5   Very sure

How do you know?

_____

_____

Would you like to be 100% sure that you have a personal relationship with God that will guarantee your passport to heaven?

_____

_____

God's power is experienced by knowing God personally and by growing in relationship with Him. God has provided the power necessary to fulfill His purposes and to carry out His mission for our lives. God is so eager to establish a personal, loving relationship with you that He has already made all the arrangements. He is patiently and lovingly waiting for you to respond to His invitation.

The major barrier that prevents us from knowing God personally is ignorance of who God is and what He has done for us. The following four principles will help you discover how to know God personally and experience the abundant life He promised.

GOD LOVES YOU AND CREATED YOU TO KNOW HIM PERSONALLY

1

a. God loves you.

"For God so loved the world, that He gave His only begotten Son, that whoever believes in Him should not perish but have eternal life."

John 3:16

b. God wants you to know Him.

"Now this is eternal life: that they may know You, the only true God, and Jesus Christ, whom You have sent."

John 17:3 (NIV)

What prevents us from knowing God personally?

WE ARE SINFUL AND SEPARATED FROM GOD, SO WE CANNOT KNOW HIM PERSONALLY OR EXPERIENCE HIS LOVE OR POWER

2

(Editor's Note: The word sin confuses a lot of people. The word sin comes from a Greek term that was used in archery. When archers shot at the target, the distance by which their arrow missed the bull's-eye was called sin. That distance represented the degree to which the archer missed the mark of perfection. When we miss God's mark of perfection, it's called sin too. And because of sin, there is a wall that separates us from a perfectly holy God. Through the years, people have tried many things to break through that wall. Money, power, and fame are just a few of the things people have tried. None of them have worked. We all fall short of God's perfection.)

a. Man is sinful.

"For all have sinned and fall short of the glory of God."

Romans 3:23

b. Man is separated.

For the wages of sin is death [spiritual separation from God].

Romans 6:23a

How can the canyon between God and man be bridged?

3 JESUS CHRIST IS THE ONLY PROVISION FOR MAN'S SIN. THROUGH HIM ALONE WE CAN KNOW GOD PERSONALLY AND EXPERIENCE GOD'S LOVE.

a. God became a man through the Person of Jesus Christ.

But the angel said to them, "Do not be afraid; for behold, I bring you good news of great joy which will be for all the people; for today in the city of David there has been born for you a Savior, who is Christ the Lord."

Luke 2:10-11

b. He died in our place.

"But God demonstrates His own love toward us in that while we were yet sinners, Christ died for us."

Romans 5:8

c. He rose from the dead.

"Christ died for our sins according to the Scriptures ... He was buried ... He was raised on the third day according to the Scriptures ... He appeared to Peter, then to the twelve. After that He appeared to more than five hundred."

1 Corinthians 15:3b-6a

d. He is the only way to God.

"Jesus said to him, 'I am the way, and the truth, and the life; no one comes to the Father but through Me.'"

John 14:6

It is not enough to know these truths ...

We Must Individually Receive Jesus Christ As Savior And Lord; Then We Can Know God Personally And Experience His Love.

4

a. We must receive Christ.

"But as many as received Him, to them He gave the right to become children of God, even to those who believe in His name."

John 1:12

b. We must receive Christ through faith.

"For by grace you have been saved through faith; and that not of yourselves, it is the gift of God; not as a result of works, so that no one may boast."

Ephesians 2:8-9

c. When we receive Christ we experience a new birth (read John 3:1-8).

d. We must receive Christ by personal invitation.

"I am the door; if anyone enters through Me, he will be saved ..."

John 10:9

Receiving Christ involves turning to God from self (repentance) and trusting Christ to come into our lives to forgive us of our sins and to make us what He wants us to be. Just to agree intellectually that Jesus Christ is the Son of God and that He died on the cross for our sins is not enough. Nor is it enough to have an emotional experience. We receive Jesus Christ by faith, as an act of our will.

These two circles represent two kinds of lives:

Which circle best represents your life?

Which circle would you like to have represent your life?

You Can Receive Christ Right Now By Faith Through Prayer

God knows your heart and is not so concerned with your words as He is with the attitude of your heart. Here is a suggested life-changing prayer:

Lord Jesus, I want to know You personally. Thank You for dying on the cross for my sins. I open the door of my life and receive You as my Savior and Lord. Thank You for forgiving me of my sins and giving me eternal life. Take control of the throne of my life. Make me the kind of person You want me to be.

If you sincerely prayed this prayer, you can know with 100% certainty that Christ is in your life and He is there to stay (Hebrews 13:5c-6). You may or may not feel like it now, but this is the most important day of your life. To remember when you joined God's family, sign and date this page.

_____	_____
Signature	Date

What Are the Results of Placing Your Faith in Jesus Christ?

The Bible says:

1. Jesus Christ came into your life (Colossians 1:27).

2. Your sins were forgiven (Colossians 1:14).

3. You became a child of God (John 1:12).

4. You received eternal life (John 5:24).

5. You have the power to pursue intimacy with God (Romans 5:5).

6. You began the great adventure, the mission, for which God created you (John 10:10, 2 Corinthians 5:17, and 1 Thessalonians 5:18).

Additional Resources on the Web

Check out our Web site at **www.familylife.com/myheart** to learn more about the *My Heart Belongs to Him* discipleship series. You'll find other resources and links for teens and their moms including:

- Information on the interactive study materials

- Testimonials from teens and moms

- Links to FamilyLife's resources that are focused on the preteen and teen years

- Additional links to a variety of information for teen gals and their moms

- A forum to share ideas and advice

Additional Resources for Your Bookshelf

Preparing Preteens and Teens for Life

Many parents are fearful as their son or daughter approaches the turbulent teen years. We need to remember that God's view of adolescence is very different from our culture's. We don't want to settle for just getting our preteens and teens through these years. The psalmist tells us that our children are like "arrows in the hands of a mighty warrior" (Psalm 127:4a).

Parents and mentors need to be proactively engaged during these vital years preceding adulthood. Our children need connection and training to develop godly convictions and character. To support parents, mentors, and church leaders in this task, FamilyLife has developed a complete series of resources with a focus on the preteen and teen season of life. With the proper preparation you can launch your "arrow" and watch it take flight!

Parenting Today's Adolescent, **by Dennis and Barbara Rainey**

FamilyLife Executive Director Dennis Rainey and his wife, Barbara, offer parents a proven plan for connecting with their adolescents and preparing them for the teen years. You will be encouraged by the Raineys' biblically based insights on peer pressure, music, grades, dating, sex, discipline, and more. Includes special single-parent sections. This pivotal book is the cornerstone for all of the other preteen and teen resources from FamilyLife.

Passport to Purity, by Dennis and Barbara Rainey

Passport to Purity gives you everything you need for a life-changing weekend with your preteen (ages 10-15). This creative, guided weekend for a father and son or a mother and daughter uses fast-paced audio teaching, dramas, projects, songs, and an adventure journal to prepare your preteen to make wise, biblical choices. You'll discuss authority, peer pressure, puberty, sex, purity, and dating. Visit www.familylife.com/passport for more information!

Teknon and the CHAMPION Warriors, by Brent Sapp

FamilyLife's new breakthrough discipleship program for sons (ages 11-16) and fathers teaches eight foundational character qualities for manhood. A dad or mentor can use this creative program to disciple a young man to stand against peer pressure, make wise choices, and positively influence others. Includes: an exciting fiction novel, *Mission Guide* (son's handbook), and *Mentor Guide* (father's handbook).

My Heart Belongs to Him series, by Nancy Butkowski and Leslie Barner

This unique, two-book discipleship series for daughters (ages 11-16) and mothers is fun, practical, and easy to use! Help your daughter discover who she is in Christ and what it means when her heart belongs to Him! Build a solid relationship with your daughter while passing on biblical convictions and values.

My Heart Belongs to Him—My Identity, Mother's Guide and Daughter's Guide

My Heart Belongs to Him—Relating With Others, Mother's Guide and Daughter's Guide

"Preparing Your Teen for Life," by Dennis and Barbara Rainey

Releasing your teen—it comes sooner than you think! That's why it's so important that you've prepared your teen for what lies ahead—a world of conflicting values and choices. This thought-provoking audio series will help you successfully guide your teen through the critical transition to adulthood.

Life Lessons, by FamilyLife (for your graduate)

Create a gift for your graduate that will be treasured forever! Life Lessons comes with a padded binder, golden baroque stationery, and simple step-by-step instructions. It includes a reproducible letter for inviting others to write meaningful notes of advice and affirmation. Contains 32 suggested topic pages in four practical categories.

These and other family resources are available by visiting FamilyLife at www.familylife.com, calling 1-800-FL-TODAY, or visiting your local Christian retailer.

About the Authors

Nancy Butkowski

Nancy Butkowski and her husband, Dan, have served with Campus Crusade for Christ for 26 years—the past 10 years they have been at FamilyLife in Little Rock, Ark. They have five daughters: Sarah, age 23;

Nicole, age 20; Janaye, age 18; Alyssa, age 15; and Sheryce, age 12. Nancy homeschooled for 14 years during which time her focus was to develop godly character in her girls, and to ground them foundationally according to biblical truths. When they got older, she and Dan chose the public school to be their laboratory for personal application.

For the past 10 years Nancy has given leadership to the Student Venture Club at public junior high and high schools, helping her daughters and many of their friends impact their campuses for Christ. She has given leadership to the teenage girls in their church youth group, and has spent the last three years teaching the content of this book to a group of mothers and daughters. She also speaks to women's groups on family-related topics.

Working closely with teenage girls, Nancy has come to understand that much of life catches them by surprise. She has a passion for being proactive in introducing girls to the real issues they will face, helping them understand the importance of godly choices to their future.

Leslie J. Barner

Leslie Barner is a staff writer for FamilyLife in Little Rock, Ark. She has served as a youth Sunday school teacher, youth group leader, youth conference and retreat speaker, and a marriage workshop leader at the God's Woman Conference (a national Christian conference for women). She has also given leadership to Bible studies for young adult women in her church. Leslie is the author of several books including *Our Legacy of Love, A Way of Hope, Xtreme Choices for Excellent Living,* and *Encouragement for the Brokenhearted Parent.*

Leslie and her husband, Aubrey, have four daughters: Desiree, Tiffany, Brittany and Krystina—one at each level of educational development from grade school to college. Working together, Leslie and her husband purpose to seize every opportunity to provide biblical instruction and guidance to their daughters. They believe it is their first and most important ministry to build godly character into their lives, to encourage them in their personal relationships with Christ, and to equip them to make an eternal difference in the lives of their peers, now and in the future.

Acknowledgments

Praise the Lord! We are so excited to see a finished product as we worked on this book series for more than three years! Even more exciting is knowing that God will use this material to make an eternal difference in the lives and relationships of mothers and daughters around the world!

We would like to thank Dennis and Barbara Rainey for believing in the validity of this project, and for giving us the opportunity to bring it to fruition. We would also like to give a special thanks to Blair Wright for his vision and direction for the project from its inception. It was his wisdom and insight that brought us—two moms with nine daughters between us—together to coauthor this book series.

A hearty thank you to Bruce Nygren for his wise editorial counsel when the series was in its earliest stages, and to Dave Boehi for his editorial wizardry and insight that gave birth to the books' user-friendly, age-group sensitive format.

Ben Colter, you have been our coach and cheerleader (there are male cheerleaders you know—smile) throughout the writing and editorial process of this series. Your product development know-how, brainstorming talents, and marketing savvy are phenomenal! We could not have done it without you!!

Bob Anderson, thank you for making sure that our books are theologically sound. Without the Word of God these books have no message.

A special thanks to Dan Butkowski, Claes Jonasson, Chuck Bostwick, and the rest of FamilyLife's Creative Resources Department for your awesome creative abilities, and for your gifts and talents in graphic arts and design. You have given this book a look and feel that will attract and bless mothers and daughters from all walks of life.

And finally, to all of the mothers and daughters who took the time to test the material before publication, we thank you from the bottom of our hearts. Because of you and your invaluable input, this book will have a life-altering and relationship-changing impact on mothers and daughters for years to come!

May God bless you all for the many unique ways in which you have invested into the lives of young women everywhere through your contribution to this series!

Nancy and Leslie

Thank you, Jesus Christ, my Lord and Savior! Without You there would be no message, no calling, no reason for life. Thank You for choosing me to mother, love, and nurture four wonderful daughters, and for uniquely equipping me for this awesome calling and cherished responsibility.

I would like to thank my husband, Aubrey, my love and my best friend. Your unconditional love, endless encouragement, and strong support continue to be my anchor. I knew that God must really love me when He gave me you!

Thank you to my four daughters, Desiree, Tiffany, Brittany, and Krystina. As a daughter myself, I stand in awe to think that you look to me in the same way I regarded my mother as "Mom" … what an awesome responsibility … what an honor! Thank you for the many special ways in which you say "I love you, Mom" every day. Whether big or small, your messages of love never go unnoticed. Thank you for your teachable spirits and for helping me discover the true meaning of godly parenting. You have been my inspiration during the writing of this book, and your life experiences have given me invaluable insight for its content.

I would like to thank my precious granddaughter, Jadeynn Nicole Guess, for giving me a little taste of heaven. You are a joy and beauty is your name!

To my parents, Lester and Geri Noble, thank you for your priceless gifts of love, encouragement, wisdom, and time. I love you!

Finally, I want to give special thanks to Blair Wright for your encouragement and support, and for your confidence in me as a writer. You have blessed my life!

Leslie

Thank you, God, for creating me with the capacity for mothering, my highest calling in life and one I have taken very seriously! Investing in the lives of my girls spiritually is the greatest contribution I will ever make in this world.

To my husband, Dan, the joy of my life, my best friend, my devoted lover, my enduring support, my constant encourager and helpmate, without you this book would not have been written. You have truly blessed my life!

I want to thank my five daughters (Sarah, Nicole, Janaye, Alyssa, and Sheryce) for putting up with all of "mom's teaching" in Student Venture, church youth group, and at home. And thank you for being my personal instructors in motherhood. Each of you is truly a gift from God and my relationship with each of you is what inspired me to write this book. I have no greater joy than knowing that my "children [are] walking in the truth, just as our Father commanded us" (2 John 4b NIV). Thank you for letting your lights shine wherever you are. You girls would make any mom proud!

My heartfelt thanks extend to all of you mothers and daughters who faithfully met at 8 a.m. on Sunday mornings over the past three years. You wrestled through many of these adolescent issues because you sought to please God with your lives. Moms, your prayer support and constant affirmation encouraged me to persevere to the end.

Nathan, thank you for letting us use your poem, "The Silver Box." To value setting aside immediate gratification for the long-term (eternal) rewards is very hard for teenagers to comprehend. Thank you for modeling before our youth your passion for God.

May God be glorified by the many lives that will be affected for eternity.

Nancy

Chapter 3

(1) Passport to Purity (Little Rock Ark.: FamilyLife, 1999), i-ii.

Session 1

(1) Leslie J. Barner, *A Way of Hope* (Little Rock, Ark.: FamilyLife, 1998).

(2) Ibid.

Session 2

(1) Debra L. Evans, *Beauty and the Best* (Colorado Springs, Colo.: Focus on the Family Publishers, 1993), 20-22.

Session 3

(1) The FamilyLife Marriage Conference Manual (Little Rock, Ark.: FamilyLife, 1999), 77-79.

Session 6

(1) Josh McDowell, *The Myths of Sex Education* (San Bernadino, Calif.: Here's Life Publishers, 1990), 8.

(2) Ibid, 10.

(3) William J. Bennett, U.S. Department of Education, January 22, 1987. Transcript of talk at the National School Board Association in Washington, D.C.

(4) Dr. James Dobson, *Life on the Edge* (Dallas, Texas: Word Publishing, 1995), 218.

(5) *USA Weekend* (a Sun newspaper, 22-24 September 1995.)

(6) *Life on the Edge*, 218.

(7) Nathan Scholl at age 19 (Little Rock, Ark.). Used by permission.

Session 8

(1) Dennis and Barbara Rainey, *Parenting Today's Adolescent* (Nashville, Tenn.: Thomas Nelson Publishers, 1998), 244-245.

My Heart Belongs to Him — My Identity